WHY I LOVE THE APOSTLE PAUL

Other Books by John Piper

Battling Unbelief
Bloodlines: Race, Cross, and the Christian
Brothers, We Are Not Professionals
The Dangerous Duty of Delight
Desiring God
Does God Desire All to Be Saved?
Don't Waste Your Life
Expository Exultation
Fifty Reasons Why Jesus Came to Die
Finally Alive
Five Points
Future Grace
God Is the Gospel
God's Passion for His Glory
A Godward Heart
A Godward Life
A Hunger for God
Lessons from a Hospital Bed
Let the Nations Be Glad!
A Peculiar Glory
The Pleasures of God
Reading the Bible Supernaturally
Seeing and Savoring Jesus Christ
Spectacular Sins
A Sweet and Bitter Providence
Taste and See
Think
This Momentary Marriage
What Jesus Demands from the World
When I Don't Desire God

WHY I LOVE THE APOSTLE PAUL

30 REASONS

JOHN PIPER

WHEATON, ILLINOIS

Why I Love the Apostle Paul: 30 Reasons

Copyright © 2019 by Desiring God Foundation

Published by Crossway
   1300 Crescent Street
   Wheaton, Illinois 60187

Cover design: Derek Thornton, Faceout Studios

Cover image: Bridgeman Images

First printing 2019

Printed in the United States of America

Trade paperback ISBN: 978-1-4335-6504-5
ePub ISBN: 978-1-4335-6507-6
PDF ISBN: 978-1-4335-6505-2
Mobipocket ISBN: 978-1-4335-6506-9

Library of Congress Cataloging-in-Publication Data

Names: Piper, John, 1946- author.
Title: Why I love the Apostle Paul : 30 reasons / John Piper.
Description: Wheaton : Crossway, 2019. | Includes bibliographical references and index.
Identifiers: LCCN 2018030461 (print) | LCCN 2018047909 (ebook) | ISBN 9781433565052 (pdf) | ISBN 9781433565069 (mobi) | ISBN 9781433565076 (epub) | ISBN 9781433565045 (tp)
Subjects: LCSH: Paul, the Apostle, Saint.
Classification: LCC BS2506.3 (ebook) | LCC BS2506.3 .P485 2019 (print) | DDC 242/.5—dc23
LC record available at https://lccn.loc.gov/2018030461

Crossway is a publishing ministry of Good News Publishers.

BP		29	28	27	26	25	24	23	22	21	20	19
15	14	13	12	11	10	9	8	7	6	5	4	3	2	1

Contents

Introduction

Liar, Lunatic, or Loved?

I have lived with the apostle Paul for over sixty years—admired him, envied him, feared him, pounded on him, memorized him, written poems about him, wept over his sufferings, soared with him, sunk to the brink of death with him, spent eight years preaching through his longest letter, imitated him. Ha—imitated him! In ten lives, I would not come close to his sufferings—or what he saw.

We Can Know the Real Paul of History

Can you really know a man who lived two thousand years ago? We have thirteen letters that he wrote and a short travelogue of his ministry—the book of Acts—written by his personal physician, Luke. My answer is yes, you can know him. And when you get to know him, you will either love him and believe him, or hate him as an impostor, or pity him as deceived, or, perhaps, simply be oblivious that you are dealing with a real man.

Perhaps you have heard the "liar, lunatic, or Lord" argument about whether Jesus was speaking truth when he claimed to be the divine Lord of the universe. He said things like, "Before Abraham was, I am" (John 8:58), and, "I and the Father are one" (John 10:30). The argument for his truth goes like this: "Christ either deceived mankind by conscious fraud, or He was Himself deluded and self-deceived, or He was Divine. There is no getting out of this trilemma. It is inexorable."[1] Liar. Lunatic. Or Lord.

In other words, the argument implies that if you find it difficult to call Jesus a liar or a lunatic, you are being led, therefore, to see him as Lord. In recent times, however, the argument has been complicated by the fact that some add a fourth possibility: legend. Liar. Lunatic. Lord. Or legend. In other words, maybe Jesus did not really say the things the New Testament records. Maybe that portrayal is legend.

There are good reasons against the view that the Jesus of the New Testament Gospels is a legend. I tried to give some of those reasons in my book *What Jesus Demands from the World*.[2] But the book in your hands is about Paul. So what's the point? The point is that no one seriously considers that Paul is a legend. Or, to be more specific, no historical scholar I am aware of seriously thinks that we do not meet the real, historical Paul in his letters. Even the most skeptical scholars, who deny Paul's authorship of five or six of his thirteen letters, believe the real, historical Paul is visible in the New Testament portrait.

Liar, Lunatic, or Authoritative Spokesman?

This means that the argument (liar, lunatic, or Lord) has a very important application to Paul. Paul does not claim to be anybody's lord. In fact, he disclaims it (2 Cor. 1:24). But he does claim to be an authoritative and truthful apostle—an autho-

---

1. John Duncan, *Colloquia Peripatetica* (Edinburgh: Edmonston & Douglas, 1873), 109.
2. John Piper, *What Jesus Demands from the World* (Wheaton, IL: Crossway, 2011), 29–36.

rized representative and spokesman—for Jesus Christ, whom he says has been raised from the dead and is reigning over the universe and will come again in glory (Gal. 1:1, 11–16; 1 Cor. 14:37–38; 15:1–9, 20–25; 1 Thess. 4:13–17).

These, of course, are crazy claims—unless they are true. So with regard to Paul we have a real trilemma. Paul was either (1) a fraud who knew his message was untrue but used religion for some ulterior reason (liar), or (2) deluded (on a par with a lunatic), or (3) an authorized and truthful spokesman for the risen Lord, Jesus Christ.

Liar, Lunatic, or Loved?

During the six decades that I have believed in Jesus, I have, from time to time, tried to step back and ask myself, as honestly as I can: Why do you believe? How can you have the confidence to build your whole life around the truth of what Paul teaches? Three years ago I wrote a whole book to answer this question— *A Peculiar Glory*.[3] But here's a short answer: I cannot with any sincerity consider Paul a liar or a lunatic. I cannot see him as a deceiver or deceived. He has won my trust.

How does that happen? It usually doesn't happen overnight. It comes from *knowing* a person. But knowing a person usually takes time. And coming to know a complex, many-faceted person may be slow and difficult. Such a person, over time, will prove to be a tangle of confusion and contradiction, or will prove to be a person of integrity and profound consistency. Paul is not confused. He is not duplicitous. He is not trying to be one of what he calls "people-pleasers" (Eph. 6:6). He does not need my approval. He doesn't fear my rejection. He does not have his

---

3. John Piper, *A Peculiar Glory: How the Christian Scriptures Reveal Their Complete Truthfulness* (Wheaton, IL: Crossway, 2016).

finger in the air to discern how the winds of culture are blowing. He is authentic.

I have found that the criteria for discerning that someone is not a lunatic or a liar overlap with the criteria for love. In other words, the traits that show a person to be mentally whole and morally honest are the same traits that awaken admiration and affection and appreciation. This is why I have written about my love for Paul. The pilgrimage of coming to love him and coming to credit him have been one pilgrimage.

Two Kinds of Love for Paul

Part of the reason why loving him and believing him have a common root is that my love is both an appreciation-love and an admiration-love. I deeply appreciate Paul's life-giving teaching, and I have huge admiration for the extraordinary traits of excellence in his life. His words have been my salvation, and his life has more than warranted those words. I owe my life to the gospel of Jesus—and no one has taken me deeper into the mysteries of the gospel than Paul. After the Lord Jesus himself, no one has won my appreciation and admiration more. And these are rooted in the very things that make a person trustworthy. They are a real validation.

That You Might See Paul as Admirable and Trustworthy

What follows in these chapters is not anything like a comprehensive overview of Paul's thought. It is highly personal, and even idiosyncratic. That is, it reflects my own peculiar pilgrimage and passions. If you love Paul and make your own list of reasons why you do, it could be very different from mine without being wrong. These different lists would not be a mark of Paul's inconsistencies. They may be a mark of his greatness.

My aim is not to establish the definitive list of Paul's authenticating traits. My aim is to commend Paul as a trustworthy witness. I believe that the reasons I love him, taken together, are a compelling case that he is not a liar or a lunatic. I want you to be deeply and joyfully persuaded that he is admirable and trustworthy and that what he writes is true.

Paul is not God. He is not the highest authority. Only Christ is the Himalayan touchstone. Christ never sinned! Paul shares not only my humanity, but also my *sinful* humanity. But, oh, what heights of greatness and Godwardness he attained—most of it through suffering! I love him for the Christ he shows me. I love him for the unsearchable riches of truth he opens to me. I love him for the constellation of his own personal excellencies, which are all the more compelling because of how diverse, even paradoxical, they are. The power of these beautiful paradoxes will be evident in the chapters that follow.

I welcome you to share my admiration—and my love—for the apostle Paul. And he would be very displeased if I did not pray that in this way, you would see and trust his Lord Jesus as your Savior, and Lord, and the supreme Treasure of your life.

PART 1

THE BEAUTIFUL
TRANSFORMATION

1

From Angry Killer to Apostle of Christ

A massive change came into Paul's life through his experience on the Damascus Road, turning him from being a killer of Christians into a lover of Christ and his people.

Paul had been a Pharisee—part of the strictest religious sect of the Jewish people (Acts 26:5). He had been schooled in his faith by Gamaliel (Acts 22:3), one of the most esteemed teachers among the Pharisees of that day (Acts 5:34). He could say in public, with no fear of contradiction: "I was advancing in Judaism beyond many of my own age among my people, so extremely zealous was I for the traditions of my fathers" (Gal. 1:14).

His pedigree for radical commitment to the strictest traditions was unsurpassed:

> . . . circumcised on the eighth day, of the people of Israel, of the tribe of Benjamin, a Hebrew of Hebrews; as to the

law, a Pharisee; as to zeal, a persecutor of the church; as to righteousness under the law, blameless. (Phil. 3:5–6)

When the first Christian martyr, Stephen, was stoned, Paul, as a young man, was there holding the coats of those who killed him (Acts 7:58). But before long he had moved from passive coat holder to aggressive persecutor.

The Event That Turned His World Upside Down

Three times, Luke, Paul's physician and travel companion and chronicler, describes the event that turned Paul's world upside down.

Breathing threats and murder against the disciples of the Lord, [Paul] went to the high priest and asked him for letters to the synagogues at Damascus, so that if he found any belonging to the Way, men or women, he might bring them bound to Jerusalem. (Acts 9:1–2)

Paul had recognized that if this menacing Christian "Way" were true, it would shatter his world. He found the meaning of his life and his "righteousness" in meticulous Mosaic law-keeping. So much so that he called himself "blameless" in this law (Phil. 3:6). Among his contemporaries, this achievement was a great "gain" (Phil. 3:7), and he outshone them all (Gal. 1:14). If the Christian Way was true—if Christ was raised from the dead—Paul had a profound sense of the implications for his own boasting. It was over.

And when Paul decided to carry his murderous persecution north to Damascus, God stepped in and turned Paul's world upside down. Paul came to believe that God had chosen him for this moment even before he was born (Gal. 1:15). Luke tells the story of Paul's crisis three times in the book of Acts (in chapters 9, 22, and 26). For example:

Now as he went on his way, he approached Damascus, and suddenly a light from heaven shone around him. And falling to the ground, he heard a voice saying to him, "Saul, Saul, why are you persecuting me?" And he said, "Who are you, Lord?" And he said, "I am Jesus, whom you are persecuting. But rise and enter the city, and you will be told what you are to do." The men who were traveling with him stood speechless, hearing the voice but seeing no one. Saul rose from the ground, and although his eyes were opened, he saw nothing. So they led him by the hand and brought him into Damascus. And for three days he was without sight, and neither ate nor drank. (Acts 9:3–9)

Then God sent a man named Ananias to explain to Paul what was happening. God had said to Ananias,

Go, for he is a chosen instrument of mine to carry my name before the Gentiles and kings and the children of Israel. For I will show him how much he must suffer for the sake of my name. (Acts 9:15–16)

Or, as Paul himself put it,

He who had set me apart before I was born, and who called me by his grace, was pleased to reveal his Son to me, in order that I might preach him among the Gentiles. (Gal. 1:15–16)

His Change Was Widely Known

The news of this conversion was stunning to the Christians in those regions because they saw the radical change that happened to Paul. Paul expresses it like this:

You have heard of my former life in Judaism, how I persecuted the church of God violently and tried to destroy it. . . . [But now those who once feared me are saying,] "He who used to persecute us is now preaching the faith he once tried to destroy." And they glorified God because of me. (Gal. 1:13, 23–24)

Paul's public life, before and after his conversion to Christ, was known by hundreds, probably thousands. His transformation, from murderer to lover, was widely known and undeniable. He is not claiming a *private* conversion experience. He is stating a public fact. His own explanation of dramatic and public change was that he had seen Jesus Christ, who had been crucified and was raised from the dead.

Jesus, Whom He Had Persecuted, Was Alive

This encounter on the road from Jerusalem to Damascus convinced Paul that Jesus was alive. And that changed everything. Jesus's offer of divine forgiveness was real. Paul received it and bowed to the absolute lordship of this risen Savior. Just as decisive for his life, he also received a mission. Nothing would ever be the same again. The persecutor was now the foremost spreader of what he had hated. He had received the gospel from the risen Christ.

I delivered to you as of first importance what I also received: that Christ died for our sins in accordance with the Scriptures, that he was buried, that he was raised on the third day in accordance with the Scriptures, and that he appeared . . . to the twelve. Then he appeared to more than five hundred brothers at one time, most of whom are still alive. . . . *Last of all . . . he appeared also to me.* For I am the least of the apostles, unworthy to be called an apostle, because I persecuted the church of God. (1 Cor. 15:3–9)

I received mercy for this reason, that in me, as the foremost [sinner], Jesus Christ might display his perfect patience as

an example to those who were to believe in him for eternal
life. (1 Tim. 1:16)

Everything that causes me to love Paul flows from this change.
Either it is all owing to a great delusion or a great hoax, or it
is worthy of my deepest amazement and admiration. The kind
of human soul that emerges from his letters is not the soul of
a deluded fanatic or a deceptive shyster. Why I believe this, is
largely what this book is about.

2

Beyond Rational Persuasion to the Revelation of Glory

Paul was converted by a blinding encounter with the brightness of the risen Lord Jesus. But when he commends the truth of the gospel in his letters, he rarely uses this undeniable experience as the warrant for why his readers should believe. He is aware that many readers will need better assurance than they can have through historical testimony.

Twice Paul referred in his letters to seeing the risen Christ on the Damascus Road, where his life was forever changed from being a persecutor of Christians to being an ambassador of the Christian faith (see chapter 1).

> Am I not free? Am I not an apostle? *Have I not seen Jesus our Lord?* Are not you my workmanship in the Lord? (1 Cor. 9:1)

[The risen Jesus] appeared to more than five hundred brothers at one time, most of whom are still alive, though some have fallen asleep. Then he appeared to James, then to all the apostles. Last of all, as to one untimely born, *he appeared also to me.* (1 Cor. 15:6–8)

Why People Should Believe Paul's Gospel

There is no doubt that Paul considered this encounter with the risen Christ, and the dramatic change in his life that followed it, as a strong reason for people to consider him a true spokesman for the Son of God.

I would have you know, brothers, that the gospel that was preached by me is not man's gospel. *For* I did not receive it from any man, nor was I taught it, but I received it through a revelation of Jesus Christ. (Gal. 1:11–12; see also Acts 22:17–21)

Notice the nature of his argument. His gospel is not merely "man's gospel," *because* he did not receive it from man. He had encountered the risen Christ.

Then he builds the argument for the truth of his gospel further with another *because* clause in Galatians 1:13: "For you have heard of my former life in Judaism, how I persecuted the church of God violently and tried to destroy it." In other words, "the change that you see in me now—risking my life for the One I used to hate—is inexplicable except for my encounter with Christ."

But What about Us Nonhistorians?

But what about the nagging questions of doubt that arise in our hearts about a gospel whose verification hangs on a distant, historical human testimony? It may be that careful historians who know how to sort through evidences and pursue long chains of reasoning can arrive at a strong probability that Paul's explanation of things is true.

But what about the ordinary person? And are we supposed to stake our lives on a strong probability? And what about the preliterate, primitive tribesman who hears a missionary tell, for the first time, the story of the gospel? Jesus bids him to take up his cross and possibly die for his faith (Luke 21:16). Is there a way he could know the truth of Paul's message with such confidence that martyrdom would not be folly?

Paul's Supernatural Defense of Truth

Here is where Paul amazes me by moving beyond his own supernatural conversion as evidence, to the intrinsic glory of the gospel itself as the ground of its truth. Listen to these profound words about how we see the truth of the gospel:

> The god of this world [Satan] has blinded the minds of the unbelievers, to keep them from *seeing the light of the gospel of the glory of Christ*, who is the image of God. For what we proclaim is not ourselves, but Jesus Christ as Lord, with ourselves as your servants for Jesus' sake. For God, who said, "Let light shine out of darkness," has *shone in our hearts to give the light of the knowledge of the glory of God* in the face of Jesus Christ. (2 Cor. 4:4–6)

First, Paul speaks of a failure to see "*the light of the gospel of the glory of Christ.*" Then he speaks of God's remedy for that failure: God has "*shone in our hearts to give the light of the knowledge of the glory of God.*" In both statements, Paul speaks of a "light." Ponder the nature of this "light." In the first statement, it shines out from the "gospel of the glory of Christ."

In the second statement, it shines out from the "knowledge of the glory of God."

In other words, this is not a *physical* or *material* light, as from the sun or from a candle. It is a *spiritual* light. It is not seen by the eyes of the head, but by what Paul sees as the eyes of the heart (Eph. 1:18). But it is not less real than physical light. This is the "light of the knowledge of the glory of God in the face of Jesus Christ." Or the "glory of Christ, who is the image of God." It is divine light shining through the story of the gospel.

How Precious That We May Know by the Sight of Glory!

This is the kind of glory the apostle John was speaking about when he said of Jesus, "We have seen his glory, glory as of the only Son from the Father, full of grace and truth" (John 1:14). But most of the Pharisees did not see it when they looked at Jesus. Hence, Jesus said, "Seeing they do not see" (Matt. 13:13).

But John saw it. And Peter saw it (Matt. 16:17). Theirs was a real seeing. And the glory of Christ was real evidence. It was a real and sure ground for faith. But it was not a physical seeing, since so many saw Jesus (and heard the gospel) and did not see this "glory" or "the light of the gospel."

I am deeply thankful that Paul was led beyond historical argumentation for the truth of the gospel. History is necessary. If there were no historical Jesus, and if there were no death for sins and resurrection from the dead, then all our faith would be in vain (1 Cor. 15:14).

But historical evidences alone do not go to the depths of our souls, where spiritual conviction rests. If we are going to live and die for Jesus, we must see his glory with the eyes of our hearts. My thankfulness to Paul at just this point is part of what I mean when I say I love him.

3

Steady in His Calling through Incomparable Sufferings

Paul was utterly devoted to the calling that the risen Christ had given him, even though it carried him into incomparable sufferings.

Many religious converts have a flash of temporary zeal, but after a while the flame burns out, and they return to the normalcy of ordinary life in this world. They choose comfort and security and live out their lives as nice people. Paul's reversal—from persecutor of Christians to radical, risk-taking promoter of Christianity—did not burn out. His life was astonishing in its single-minded devotion to the person and the cause he came to love—Jesus Christ and salvation by grace.

The Beauty of Single-Mindedness in a Great Cause

I love single-mindedness. I love to see an entire life devoted to one great thing. To me it is beautiful when a human soul, instead of flitting from one interest to another, sets a course of life and stays on it till the end. Of course, this is praiseworthy only if the goal is worth a lifetime of focus. In a few places, Paul distills the passion of his life into a sentence. For example:

> I do not account my life of any value nor as precious to myself, if only I may finish my course and the ministry that I received from the Lord Jesus, to testify to the gospel of the grace of God. (Acts 20:24)

I summarize this magnificent sentence as follows: *better to lose your life than to waste it.* And for Paul, not wasting his life meant staying on one single course all the way to the end—the course of "testifying to the gospel of the grace of God." He uses this same word *course*, translated *race*, in his farewell words at the end of his life:

> I have fought the good fight, I have finished the *race*, I have kept the faith. Henceforth there is laid up for me the crown of righteousness. (2 Tim. 4:7–8)

He made it. All the way to the end. Is this not a beautiful thing, when a man has a great, worthy, single passion in life and burns for it all the way to the end? At the end, as he came to Rome for the last time, even then, as an older man, he was planning to go to Spain because there was a specific angle to his passion for the "gospel of the grace of God." Namely, to go where the gospel hadn't gone:

> I make it my ambition to preach the gospel, not where Christ has already been named, lest I build on someone else's foundation. (Rom. 15:20)

As far as we know, he didn't make it to Spain. But I would rather see a man die abruptly, on his way to one last conquest, than to see him drift off course into the comforts of old age.

The Passion in All His Passions

Perhaps the expression of Paul's single passion that has captured my heart most deeply is the one found in Philippians 1:20. Whether Paul says that his single course is to testify to the gospel of the grace of God or that his ambition is to preach that gospel where it's never been preached—in either case, in and under and through that single life passion was the ultimate goal of living and dying *that Jesus Christ be magnified in Paul's body*. This was the life passion unifying all his strategic aims:

> It is my eager expectation and hope that I will not be at all ashamed, but that with full courage now as always Christ will be honored [or magnified] in my body, whether by life or by death.

Every dream, every plan, every strategy, every movement, every message—with this one all-unifying passion: "that Christ be magnified in my body, whether by life or by death."

Through Unremitting Suffering

But it is not just the singleness of his passion and the steadfastness of his focus that win my admiration and love; it is the fact that in this unwavering commitment to his God-given mission, his sufferings were unremitting and almost unbearable—and he still kept to the course. To be sure, it is noteworthy when anyone holds fast to a single glorious cause in life. But it is staggering to do this through unremitting suffering.

I choose the word *unremitting* carefully. At the time of Paul's conversion, Jesus said of him: "I will show him how much he must suffer for the sake of my name" (Acts 9:16). And then, when Paul describes his life of trials, they sound not only unremitting, but as if they come from every direction:

[I have served Christ] with far greater labors, far more imprisonments, with countless beatings, and often near death. Five times I received at the hands of the Jews the forty lashes less one. Three times I was beaten with rods. Once I was stoned. Three times I was shipwrecked; a night and a day I was adrift at sea; on frequent journeys, in danger from rivers, danger from robbers, danger from my own people, danger from Gentiles, danger in the city, danger in the wilderness, danger at sea, danger from false brothers; in toil and hardship, through many a sleepless night, in hunger and thirst, often without food, in cold and exposure. And, apart from other things, there is the daily pressure on me of my anxiety for all the churches. (2 Cor. 11:23–28)

If you read that with a warmhearted sense of imagination and empathy, you can easily come to tears. Remember, he was not married. And though he had many close friends, how alone he must have felt much of the time. Picture him late at night, recovering alone from wounds, when others were cared for by a wife.

A Sane Man Knows When He Is Speaking Like a Madman

Of course, maybe your response is not one of imaginative empathy and tears, but one of suspicion. Perhaps you say, "This list of sufferings sounds like bragging." You would be onto something. It was a kind of bragging. And you should ask (I certainly have), "Why would that be admirable?" Why wouldn't this be evidence that he is losing his bearings and talking like a self-consumed madman?

Here's my answer. False apostles were trying to undermine Paul's work in Corinth, where he sent that list of sufferings. They boasted of great credentials. So Paul says—and he knows this is very risky!—"Are they servants of Christ? I am a better one—I am talking *like a madman*" (2 Cor. 11:23).

In other words, only fools brag like this. So, yes! He says it right out loud: "I have been a fool! You forced me to it, for I ought to have been commended by you. For I was not at all inferior to these super-apostles, even though I am nothing" (2 Cor. 12:11). That's risky.

And I love him for taking the risk. Because I know from thirteen letters that this man is not a craven egotist who needs propping up through praise or pity. The difference between a sane man and a madman is that when the sane man talks like a madman, he knows it, and names it. Why does he take the risk of talking like a madman? Is it "because I do not love you? God knows I do!" (2 Cor. 11:11).

Yes. He loves them. That is the meaning of these sufferings. I too feel loved by this "madman" and his list of sorrows in the pursuit of his single passion—magnifying Christ in life and death. How can I not love him in return?

4

Unwavering Love for Those Who Scourged Him

Paul did not allow his suffering at the hands of the Jews to turn his heart against his own beloved Jewish people.

In the long list of Paul's sufferings (2 Cor. 11:23–33), the one that moves me most and makes me cringe with each added instance is the one he describes by saying, "Five times I received at the hands of the Jews the forty lashes less one" (v. 24). Three things make this seem to me the most horrible.

Why the Five Scourgings Were Horrible

First, there is the sheer number of lashes—thirty-nine in each flogging. Second, those thirty-nine lashes happened five times, presumably on the same scarred back. Third, it was the Jews— his own kindred, as he calls them elsewhere (Rom. 9:3)—who were doing the scourging.

Imagine with me such a flogging. Count the strokes. Surely the flesh would eventually break open even if the flogger tried to be lenient. And there is no indication that these floggings were an attempt to be lenient. They were performed by Paul's Jewish adversaries. This was the standard way of punishing in connection with the synagogues. Jesus had said it would happen.

> Beware of men, for they will deliver you over to courts and *flog you in their synagogues*. (Matt. 10:17)

> I send you prophets and wise men and scribes, . . . and *some you will flog in your synagogues* and persecute from town to town. (Matt. 23:34)

The Old Testament had prescribed the maximum stripes for the legal flogging of a criminal. It should be proportionate to the crime, but in any case not more than forty:

> If the guilty man deserves to be beaten, the judge shall cause him to lie down and be beaten in his presence with a number of stripes in proportion to his offense. Forty stripes may be given him, but not more, lest, if one should go on to beat him with more stripes than these, your brother be degraded in your sight. (Deut. 25:2–3)

There was another reason why forty lashes were not to be surpassed: this was not to be a death sentence. Nevertheless, at least one Jewish source warns about the possibility of a victim dying during or after the full scourging (m. Makkot 3:14). These were not light strokes.

Therefore, Paul was not being treated leniently. The scourging was deadly, and he was receiving the maximum number allowed. Most scholars agree that only thirty-nine were given instead of forty in order to protect the synagogue against transgressing the legal maximum in case there was a miscount.

These five scourgings were not a marginal part of Paul's life. By the end of all five scourgings, his back must have been a tangle of raw, tender, stiff scar tissue that probably made his movements painful.

Therefore, I ask you again to imagine the effect these thirty-nine lashes would have on the back. Then imagine the healing process in an era with no antibiotics and certainly no plastic surgery to adjust the scar tissue. Then imagine it happening the second time on the same back. The healing is slower. Then imagine a third time. The healing is slower yet, as the scar tissue remains tender and never quite knits properly. Then imagine the fourth time on the same scarred, partially healed back. And finally, imagine Paul being tied down a fifth time.

The reason I say, "Try to imagine this," is not mainly to create a sense of the physical agony, but to create a sense of what you might feel toward God and your adversaries, the Jewish people. We have already seen how Paul refused to be angry at God, though he knew that one word from God, and his persecutors would be struck blind (which actually happened on the island of Cyprus, Acts 13:11)—something God chose not to do during these five scourgings.

Unwavering Love for Those Who Scourged Him

That is amazing enough—that Paul would see a second, then a third, then a fourth, then a fifth flogging coming, and not curse God. But add to this amazement that he never stopped loving his Jewish people, who actually did the flogging. If this happened over and over when he preached in the synagogues of the Roman world, why would he keep going back? There are two main reasons.

The first reason is that the gospel of grace to which he was totally committed was designed by God to be *"to the Jew first* and also to the Greek." Paul wrote to the Roman Christians, "I am not ashamed of the gospel, for it is the power of God for salvation to everyone who believes, to the Jew first and also to the Greek" (Rom. 1:16). Paul went to the synagogues first, and then he turned to the Gentiles.

The second reason is more personal. He *loved* his Jewish kinsmen. Their rejection of the gospel was a spiritual torment to him. This sorrow was a greater incentive to reach his kinsmen with the gospel than his floggings were a disincentive. He wrote:

> I have great sorrow and unceasing anguish in my heart. For I could wish that I myself were accursed and cut off from Christ for the sake of my brothers, my kinsmen according to the flesh. . . . My heart's desire and prayer to God for them is that they may be saved. (Rom. 9:2–3; 10:1)

When I see Paul enduring five floggings of thirty-nine lashes each "at the hands of the Jews," and then see him returning every time to these loved ones, as he says, "that by all means I might save some" (1 Cor. 9:22), I stand in awe of his love—his love for Christ and the gospel, and his love for his people.

Loving Jesus in Paul

I see Jesus in this man. For Jesus said, "Love your enemies, do good to those who hate you, bless those who curse you, pray for those who abuse you" (Luke 6:27–28). And then Jesus did it on the cross. Paul said, "When reviled, we bless; when persecuted, we endure; when slandered, we entreat" (1 Cor. 4:12–13). He saw his scars as the very marks of Jesus's dying love: "We are . . . always carrying in the body the death of Jesus, so that the life of Jesus may also be manifested in our bodies" (2 Cor. 4:8–10). For this I stand in awe of Paul, and love him.

5

Unshakable Contentment
Whether Abased or Abounding

Paul did not minimize or make light of his sufferings, but he was not embittered by them. Instead, he found contentment in God's merciful purposes through them.

I am drawn to people who suffer without murmuring. Especially when they believe in God but never get angry with him or criticize him. It seems to me that not murmuring is one of the rarest traits in the world. And when it is combined with a deep faith in God—who could alter our painful circumstances, but doesn't—it has a beautiful God-trusting, God-honoring quality that makes it all the more attractive. Paul was like that.

Brought to the Brink of Death

Paul tells of the time when his faith was put to the test in a way that brought him to the brink of despair and death:

> We were so utterly burdened beyond our strength that
> we despaired of life itself. Indeed, we felt that we had
> received the sentence of death. But that was to make us
> rely not on ourselves but on God who raises the dead. He
> delivered us from such a deadly peril, and he will deliver
> us. On him we have set our hope that he will deliver us
> again. (2 Cor. 1:8–10)

Three things are remarkable here. First is the severity of the suffering: "We felt that we had received the sentence of death." Second, there is purpose or design in this suffering: "That was to
make us rely not on ourselves but on God who raises the dead."
Third, this purpose was *God's* purpose. It could not have been
Satan's, since Satan certainly does not want Paul to rely on God.

So the truth that Paul believed about his suffering—no matter how severe—was that it came ultimately with God's purpose, and the purpose was that Paul would trust himself less
and trust God more, every moment of his life, especially as
death approached.

A Key to Not Murmuring

This, it seems, is how Paul could be free from murmuring in
his suffering. He knew God was in charge of it and that God's
purposes were totally for Paul's good. Paul fleshes this truth out
in several other places:

> We rejoice in our sufferings, knowing that suffering pro-
> duces endurance, and endurance produces character, and
> character produces hope, and hope does not put us to shame,
> because God's love has been poured into our hearts through
> the Holy Spirit who has been given to us. (Rom. 5:3–5)

Again, the basis of Paul's freedom from murmuring—indeed the presence of his *rejoicing*—was his confidence that

God was at work doing something crucial in Paul—producing endurance and God-saturated hope.

Suffering without Earthly Life on the Other Side

But what about suffering that leads only to death and not to a new chapter of life on earth where reliance on God (2 Cor. 1:9) and deepened character and hope (Rom. 5:4) might be increased? Paul was keenly aware of this question and gave his answer in 2 Corinthians 4:16–18:

> We do not lose heart. Though our outer self is wasting away, our inner self is being renewed day by day. For this light momentary affliction is preparing for us an eternal weight of glory beyond all comparison, as we look not to the things that are seen but to the things that are unseen. For the things that are seen are transient, but the things that are unseen are eternal.

The issue here is the gradual wasting away of human life—through affliction and sickness and aging. In other words, the next chapter after this suffering is not a season of greater faith and hope on earth. The next chapter is heaven.

So is there any point in the increased suffering that comes with the approach of death? How do those of us who have only a few years left not murmur at our aches and pains and the onrush of death? Paul's answer is that this life's afflictions—if we endure them by trusting Christ—actually produce greater measures of glory in heaven. "This . . . affliction is preparing for us an eternal weight of glory."

Amazing Contentment in Hard Times and Easy Times

Therefore, even though Paul's life was one of seemingly unremitting sufferings (2 Cor. 11:23–33, see chapter 3), there is scarcely a hint of murmuring, and none against God. He could get angry at destructive error and its teachers (Gal. 1:8–9; 5:12). And he could express his pressures and burdens (2 Cor. 11:28). Nevertheless, his contentment through it all was unusual.

He said he had learned the *secret* of contentment:

> I have learned in whatever situation I am to be content. I know how to be brought low, and I know how to abound. In any and every circumstance, I have learned the secret of facing plenty and hunger, abundance and need. I can do all things through him who strengthens me. (Phil. 4:11–13)

This "secret" seemed to be the all-satisfying presence and worth of Christ (Phil. 3:8), together with the confidence Paul felt in the merciful sovereignty of God that would work all things for his good (Phil. 1:12; Rom. 8:28). Watching Paul maintain his humble, God-dependent, Christ-cherishing contentment through all his sufferings causes me to stand in awe of this man.

PART 2

LOVING THE MAN WHO SHAPED MY LIFE

6

Magnifying Christ through a Satisfying Death

Paul led me out of one of the greatest unresolved tensions in my life and into the discovery of what I call "Christian Hedonism," which has guided and shaped my life for fifty years.

When I was in college, I lived with an unresolved tension in my Christian faith. On the one hand, I had learned from my parents and from the Bible that I was supposed to live for the glory of God. "Whether you eat or drink, or whatever you do, do all to the glory of God" (1 Cor. 10:31). This meant that my motive in all I did was supposed to be to help people see the reality of God's greatness and beauty.

On the other hand, I wanted to be happy. I could not turn off this desire. It was as natural as getting hungry between meals. As the Scottish preacher Thomas Boston said three hundred years ago:

> Consider what man is. He is, (1.) A creature that desires
> happiness, and cannot but desire it. The desire of happiness
> is woven into his nature, and cannot be eradicated. It is
> as natural for him to desire it as it is to breathe. (2.) He is
> not self-sufficient: he is conscious to himself that he wants
> many things, and therefore he is ever seeking something
> without himself in order to be happy.[1]

The unresolved tension was that I felt that these two motives
were at odds with each other. It seemed to me that if I was
motivated by the desire for my own happiness, the aim to
glorify God was compromised. After all, didn't Jesus say,
"If anyone would come after me, let him deny himself"
(Mark 8:34)?

From Golden Nuggets to Links of Steel

But soon after I graduated from college, in my first year of seminary, I began to study the letters of Paul in a way that I had
never done before. Until then I saw the Bible mainly as a collection of golden nuggets of truth and wisdom. Each day I would
go to this chest of gold and find a nugget or two and carry them
around during the day.

But almost overnight I discovered the explosive truth that
the biblical authors, especially Paul, do not just assemble nuggets, or even a string of pearls. Paul, more rigorously than any
other, forges solid links in a steel chain of unbreakable logic.
I know *logic* does not sound explosive or life giving to many
people. But let me try to show you why this was utterly life
changing for me, and how it provided the key that resolved the
tension I had lived with for years.

---

1. Thomas Boston, *An Illustration of the Doctrines of the Christian Religion*,
vol. 1, *The Whole Works of Thomas Boston*, ed. Samuel M'Millan (Aberdeen:
George & Robert King, 1848), 16.

The Liberating Chain Begins to Form

Come with me to Paul's letter to the Philippians. In the first chapter, he says:

> It is my eager expectation and hope that I will not be at all ashamed, but that with full courage now as always Christ will be [magnified] in my body, whether by life or by death. For to me to live is Christ, and to die is gain. (Phil. 1:20–21)[2]

Notice that Paul expresses the first half of my life tension, namely, his passion to live for the glory of God. He says that his "eager expectation and hope" is that Christ (who is the fullest revelation of God) would be "magnified" in his body. That is what I always thought I should live for—to show others how magnificent *God* is, as he is revealed in Christ. "Do all to the glory of God."

Formerly, I might have thought of this as a beautiful nugget to put in the pocket of my memory for the day, and to admire, and to pray that it would become a reality in my life. But now I was being forced by a wise teacher to see this not as a nugget but as a link in a chain of reasoning. Follow it with me.

The Argument Emerges

As soon as Paul says in verse 20 that Christ will be magnified in his body "whether by life or by death," he adds verse 21 and gives the *basis* for this. Notice the word *for* at the beginning of verse 21 (a sure sign that a chain is being forged!). These little words and phrases—like *for* and *because* and *since* and *therefore* and *in order that*—I had once paid little attention to.

---

2. The ESV reads "honored," but in this chapter, and throughout the book, I have supplied my translation of the Greek *megalunthēsetai* as "magnified."

But now I began to see that for Paul, these were the words that forge the connections and turn nuggets into links in a chain.

As I tried to think through this connection between verses 20 and 21, I noticed that the words "by life or by death" in verse 20 correspond to the words "to *live* is Christ, and to *die* is gain" in verse 21. So it became clear that the *for* (= *because*) at the beginning of verse 21, and the reference to life and death in both verses, means that Paul is explaining in verse 21 how it is that Christ will be shown as magnificent in his body both in dying and in living.

So how does the argument work? If you see this, and it penetrates to the center of your soul the way it did for me, you'll never be the same again. Let's just focus on the connection between *death* in verse 20 and the words *to die* in verse 21.[3] How does it work that Paul's *dying* will make Christ look magnificent?

Here's what he says: "My eager expectation is that Christ will be *magnified* by my death, *because* for me to die is *gain*." Do you begin to see how his death would make Christ look magnificent? He is saying, "My death will make Christ look magnificent *because* for me to die is *gain*." So the key to showing Christ as magnificent is to experience death as gain! Or, to say it another way, the key *to magnifying Christ in dying is to experience death as satisfying*.

How Can Death Be Satisfying?

Death as satisfying? This is shocking. When you die, your spouse is gone, sex is gone, the children are gone, the dream retirement is gone, hobbies are gone, and, until the resurrection, the body, with all its pleasures, is gone. So what does Paul

---

3. I have explained elsewhere how the other pair—life and live—serves to magnify Christ. See https://www.desiringgod.org/interviews/to-live-is-christ-what-does -that-mean.

mean that all this *loss* can be called *gain*? He gives the answer in verses 22–23:

> If I am to live in the flesh, that means fruitful labor for me. Yet which I shall choose I cannot tell. I am hard pressed between the two. *My desire is to depart and be with Christ, for that is far better.*

Dying, for Paul, means being with Christ. And he says that this is *far better* than his present life. When Paul compares all the pleasures that are confined to this physical world with the pleasure of being with Christ face-to-face, he calls death *gain*, even though it takes away all those earthly pleasures. Death gives him a closer experience of Christ. This is gain. Just like he says in Philippians 3:8: "I count everything as loss because of the surpassing worth of knowing Christ Jesus my Lord."

Unlocking the Tension of My Life

So, according to this chain of logic from verses 20–23, how is Christ shown to be magnificent in our dying? Paul's answer is that Christ is shown to be magnificent in our dying when we experience him as more satisfying than all the pleasures that life in this world could give. Do you see how astonishing this was for me? It gave me the key that unlocked the tension between my desire that God be glorified and my desire to be satisfied.

This was the birth of what I call "Christian Hedonism"— the way I have tried to live my life for the last fifty years. I have put it in a rhyming motto: *God is most glorified in us when we are most satisfied in him.* If you have been tracking with me, you can see that this did not come out of the blue. It came out of following the logic of this great apostle. The logic in Philippians 1:20–23 says, in essence: *Christ is most magnified in me when I am most satisfied in him, especially through suffering and death.* That is what I mean by Christian Hedonism.

And what a liberating relief it was! It resolved the tension in my heart. I saw that God's passion to be glorified and my passion to be satisfied were *not* alternatives. Paul said that Christ is magnified not *instead of* my being satisfied in him, but *by means of* my being satisfied in him. Did you get that? Not *instead of* but *by means of.* This changed everything.

My satisfaction in Christ above all this world, at the point of suffering and death, is what makes Christ look magnificent—all-satisfying. Therefore, my pursuit of satisfaction—my pursuit of happiness—is not just permitted. It is mandatory, because glorifying God is mandatory. And you cannot glorify God in your heart if your heart does not find God more satisfying than everything else.

Almost Too Good to Be True

This was almost too good to be true. I not only *may,* but I *must,* pursue happiness—in God. I began to see this all over the Bible. It was commanded: "Delight yourself in the LORD" (Ps. 37:4). "Be glad in the LORD" (Ps. 32:11). "Rejoice in the Lord" (Phil. 3:1). If we stop pursuing this joy in God, we will betray him. We will belie his worth.

It is not noble to seek God with no desire to delight in him. It is an insult. As if we should say, "God, you are more precious than gold, but I don't want to treasure you." Or, "God, you are sweeter than honey, but I don't want to savor you." Or, "You are the fountain of life and a river of delights, but I don't want to be satisfied in you."

No! That may sound like self-denial. But it is not the self-denial Christ called for. It is God-denial. The self-denial Christ called for is to deny ourselves the two-bit, fleeting pleasures of sin, so that we can have full pleasures in God forever. The reason for self-denial that Jesus gives is this: "Whoever loses his life for my sake and the gospel's will save it" (Mark 8:35). Save it! For what? For this: "In your presence there is fullness of joy; at your right hand are pleasures forevermore" (Ps. 16:11).

My tension was resolved. My quest was over. And it was this amazing apostle Paul who had been my guide to the greatest discovery of my life. Perhaps you can begin to feel the affection I have for him. No one in my life, besides Jesus himself, has led me into treasures of life-changing truth like this man.

7

Love for People as the Overflow of Joy in God

> Paul freed me from the fear that I was minimizing the worth of God or of people by pursuing my own joy in doing good for others. He showed me what love really is.

It was a thrilling discovery when Paul showed me how glorifying God and satisfying my soul are not at odds. More clearly than any other writer in the Bible, Paul opened up the truth that God is most glorified in me when I am most satisfied in him. I told that story in chapter 6.

But there is a second chapter to that story that makes my thankfulness to Paul all the sweeter. I owe to him, more than to anyone else, another crucial, life-changing discovery. If the first discovery was how to resolve the tension between the desire to glorify God and the desire to be happy, the second discovery was how to resolve the tension between the desire to be happy in God and the desire to love other people.

Another Unresolved Tension

Can you really love people if, in the very act of doing them good, you are seeking the fullness of your own joy? After all, it was Paul himself who said, "Love . . . does not seek its own" (1 Cor. 13:4–5 NASB). And in another place, "Let no one seek his own good, but the good of his neighbor" (1 Cor. 10:24). And again, "We . . . have an obligation to bear with the failings of the weak, and not to please ourselves" (Rom. 15:1). So how can you claim to love people if, in the very act of loving them, you are seeking your own joy?

This question felt just as urgent as the first one about how to glorify God while seeking my own joy. Jesus had said that the "first and great" commandment is to love God. But he also said that the commandment to love our neighbor is "like it" (Matt. 22:39). So the question of how to love people out of a heart that could not stop wanting to be happy—indeed, a heart that *dare not* stop wanting to be happy, lest God be dishonored by my failing to be happy in him—that question was just as urgent as any.

So how does the pursuit of joy in God relate to love for other people? Paul showed me that genuine, Spirit-awakened joy in God does not hinder love for people but in fact *overflows* with love for people. It has a built-in impulse to expand. Joy in God grows as it's extended into the lives of other people so they can share in it.

Again, Paul Points the Way

Paul gives us the most explicit illustration of this in the New Testament. It's found in 2 Corinthians 8:1–2, where Paul is seeking to motivate love in the Corinthians by pointing to the Macedonian Christians and the amazing way they had shown love.

> We want you to know, brothers, about the grace of God that has been given among the churches of Macedonia, for in a severe test of affliction, *their abundance of joy* and

their extreme poverty have *overflowed in a wealth of generosity* on their part. . . . I say this not as a command, but to prove by the earnestness of others that *your love also* is genuine. (2 Cor. 8:1–2, 8)

Note carefully that the "abundance of joy" in the hearts of the Macedonians was not owing to comfortable circumstances. They were in "extreme poverty" and "a severe test of affliction." Their abundance of joy was owing to the "grace of God" that had been "given" (v. 1). Their sins were forgiven. The wrath of God had been replaced with the divine smile of everlasting favor. Guilt was gone. Hell was closed. Heaven was open. The Spirit was indwelling. Hope had exploded in their hearts. All of this because of Christ, when they deserved none of it. The grace of God had been given (v. 1).

This "abundance of joy" became a fountain of love for people. It could not be clearer: "Their abundance of joy . . . overflowed in a wealth of generosity" (v. 2). This was love. He called it that in verse 8: ". . . that your *love* also is genuine." So Paul's definition of genuine, God-exalting love would be this: *Love is the overflow of joy in God that meets the needs of others.*

Seeking Happiness in God for the Sake of Loving People

This is more profound than what first meets the eye. Paul is *not* saying, "True happiness requires love for people." That's true. An unloving person will not be happy in the long run. But this is an oversimplification that misses the crucial point. The point is not that in order to have the truest pleasure we must love people. Rather, the point is that when joy in God overflows into the lives of others in the form of generosity, that overflow of joy *is* love. Or to say it another way: we do not merely seek to love in order to be happy, but we seek to be happy in God in order to love. It was their "abundance of joy" that overflowed in love (v. 2).

This thought seemed so radical to me that I wanted to check myself by testing it with the rest of Scripture. Is it true that my joy is that closely connected with my love for people? What I found was a stream of biblical commands to:

- *love* kindness, not just *do* it (Mic. 6:8);
- do acts of mercy *with cheerfulness* (Rom. 12:8);
- *joyfully* suffer loss in the service of prisoners (Heb. 10:34);
- be a *cheerful* giver (2 Cor. 9:7);
- make *our joy* the joy of others (2 Cor. 2:3);
- tend the flock of God willingly and *eagerly* (1 Pet. 5:2); and
- keep watch over souls *with joy* (Heb. 13:17).

To me this was amazing. We are not dealing here with something marginal or clever. This really is soul piercing and radically life changing: the pursuit of authentic love for people includes the pursuit of joy, because joy in God is an essential component of authentic love. This is vastly different from saying, "Let's all be loving because it will make us happy." This is saying, "Let's all seek to be so full of joy in God that it overflows in sacrificial love to other people."

Love Endures Because Joy Endures through Suffering

That word *sacrificial* might sound paradoxical. If we are overflowing in joy to others, and our joy is expanding by drawing others into it, then why talk of sacrifice? The reason is that the path of greatest joy in this life is often the path of great suffering. In the age to come, after Jesus returns, all pain will be gone. But not yet. In this life, love will often demand suffering. It may, in fact, demand that we lay down our lives. But Paul sets the pace for us when he says, "I *rejoice* in my sufferings for your sake" (Col. 1:24). "In all our affliction, I am overflowing with *joy*" (2 Cor. 7:4). "We *rejoice* in our sufferings" (Rom. 5:3).

There are reasons for this strange and wonderful kind of joy that survives and even thrives in affliction. One reason is that Jesus taught us, "It is more blessed to give than to receive" (Acts 20:35). The overflow to others is enriching to us. Another reason is that even though "some of you they will put to death," in the end "not a hair of your head will perish" (Luke 21:16, 18). Jesus had said, "Everyone who lives and believes in me shall never die" (John 11:26). The world thinks we die. But Jesus takes us so immediately into his care that there is no break in life. A third reason is the promise "your reward is great in heaven" (Matt. 5:12). Finally, the greatest act of love that was ever performed was sustained by joy in God: "[Look] to Jesus, . . . who for the joy that was set before him endured the cross" (Heb. 12:2).

This is why, during my thirty-three years as a pastor, the signature text we came back to again and again was 2 Corinthians 6:10: "as sorrowful, yet always rejoicing." Always. Rejoicing *at the same time* as sorrowing. Not just sequentially. Simultaneously. Loving others does not have to wait till sorrow passes, because joy does not wait.

And during those thirty-three years, the signature song that the pastoral staff would sing again and again was "It Is Well with My Soul":

> When peace like a river attendeth my way,
> When sorrows like sea billows roll;
> Whatever my lot, thou hast taught me to say,
> "It is well, it is well with my soul."

Genuine love makes many sacrifices for the beloved. There is much pain and many sorrows. But in Christ there is no *ultimate* sacrifice. To be sure, Jesus calls for self-denial. But his argument for self-denial (as we saw in chapter 6) is "whoever loses his life for my sake and the gospel's *will save it*" (Mark 8:35). On the other side of self-denial—even death—is everlasting joy in the presence of God.

Begrudging Generosity Does Not Make People Feel Loved

I have never met anyone who is offended because the sacrifices we make for their good bring us joy. In fact, merely dutiful "love"—or worse, begrudging "love"—does not make people feel loved. It makes them feel like a burden. I am sure, therefore, that Paul would agree with the writer to the Hebrews when he tells his hearers to let the leaders keep watch over them "*with joy* and not with groaning, for that would be of no advantage to you" (Heb. 13:17). Begrudging ministry is of *no advantage* to the people. Or to put it positively, finding joy in caring for people is a great advantage to them. It is love.

This is surely why Paul said to the Corinthians, "I felt sure of all of you, that my joy would be the joy of you all" (2 Cor. 2:3). Yes! If you come to me and want me to experience joy— that is, if you want to love me—come with joy. And the best joy of all is joy in God. Bring me that. Overflow on me with that. I will feel loved. And you will be glad.

So Paul has done it again. He not only showed me how my pursuit of God's glory and my pursuit of happiness fit together (chapter 6), but he also showed me how that unquenchable desire for happiness fits together with loving people. *Genuine, Christ-exalting, Spirit-empowered, sacrificial love for people is the overflow of joy in God that expands by meeting the needs of others.* How can I not love the man who, after the Lord Jesus, showed me, more clearly than anyone else, the beauty of such a way of life?

8

From Rabid Ethnic Arrogance to Herald of Deepest Reconciliation

Although he was a "Hebrew of Hebrews," with an impeccable religious and ethnic pedigree as a Jew and a Pharisee, he passionately worked for reconciliation and unity among Christians of different classes and ethnic backgrounds.

I didn't always love Paul for his work of reconciliation. There are years in my past for which I am ashamed—years of racism when I was so in the thrall of my Southern culture of the 1950s and 1960s that I could not see what was staring up at me from the pages of Paul's letters. I don't say it that way to lessen my own guilt, as though I could somehow blame my blindness on culture. I was a more-than-willing accomplice in the racial ugliness of those days. I've told the whole story in *Bloodlines: Race, Cross, and the Christian*.[1]

---

1. John Piper, *Bloodlines: Race, Cross, and the Christian* (Wheaton, IL: Crossway, 2011).

Paul, My Liberator

But there came a time when the scales began to fall away. (I say *began* so as not to imply the total absence of blinders still.) Of course, it was the work of no mere man. "Never since the world began has it been heard that anyone opened the eyes of a man born blind" (John 9:32). No. This was a gracious, sovereign work of Jesus by his Spirit. But, as always, he used a human agent. He used human words. In fact, he used the apostle Paul.

Paul could help me because he had at one time been as prejudiced against Gentiles as I was against African Americans. Paul called himself "a Hebrew of Hebrews" (Phil. 3:5). He considered his ethnic and religious pedigree, with the zeal of a persecutor and the blamelessness of a Pharisee (Phil. 3:6), to be almost without peer in his generation (Gal. 1:14). He would have said with his fellow Jewish apostle Peter, "You yourselves know how unlawful it is for a Jew to associate with or to visit anyone of another nation" (Acts 10:28).

But then something happened. It was both devastating and liberating. It devastated every ground of boasting that Paul had. And it liberated him for the experience of a new humanity that was not defined by race or ethnicity or cultural custom. He tallied up all the pride and gain he had achieved through ethnic and religious distinctives and called it *excrement* in comparison to Christ.

> But whatever gain I had, I counted as loss for the sake of Christ. Indeed, I count everything as loss because of the surpassing worth of knowing Christ Jesus my Lord. For his sake I have suffered the loss of all things and count them as excrement, in order that I may gain Christ. (Phil. 3:7–8, my translation)

Penetrating to the Revolution of the Cross

By God's illuminating grace, Paul penetrated to the ethnic achievements of the cross of Christ. Here's what happened when Christ died:

> In Christ Jesus you [Gentiles] who once were far off have been brought near *by the blood of Christ*. For he himself is our peace, who has *made us both one* [Jew and Gentile] and has broken down *in his flesh* the dividing wall of hostility by abolishing the law of commandments expressed in ordinances, that he might *create in himself one new man* in place of the two, so making peace, and might *reconcile us both to God in one body through the cross*, thereby killing the hostility. . . . For through him *we both have access in one Spirit to the Father*. (Eph. 2:13–18)

"By the blood of Christ . . . in his flesh . . . through the cross. . . . He made us both one . . . breaking down the hostility . . . creating one new man . . . reconciling us both to God . . . with access together in one Spirit to the Father." These are revolutionary words. In that day or in any day. In Rwanda, or Cambodia, or Iran, or India, or in South Carolina.

And they are not first and foremost political words, or social justice words, or civil rights words, but gospel words. They are blood-bought, Christ-exalting, heaven-opening words. They are the triumphant fruit of the death of the Son of God. To love the old rugged cross is to love the fruit of the cross. Christ died to create "one new man." Christ died to remove the "wall of hostility." Christ died to "be our peace." Christ died so that there would *not* be multiple segregated accesses to the Father, but that "we would both [name your ethnic rivalry] have access in one Spirit to the Father."

Not for the World First, but for the Church

And all of this is "in Christ"—in Christ you have been brought near. This is not first a mandate for secular culture. This is first a mandate for Christians—those who are *in Christ*—a mandate for how we relate to each other. In the church, this is the way it should be. Christian exiles and sojourners are not responsible for making unbelievers act like believers. But, oh, how responsible we are to love what Christ died to achieve, and to act like it!

Here "in Christ," here in the church, Paul says in Colossians 3:11, "There is not Greek and Jew, circumcised and uncircumcised, barbarian, Scythian, slave, free; but Christ is all, and in all." Because Christ is *worth* all, and is *in* all, racial and ethnic differences should no longer create hostility or suspicion or distrust or disrespect or disregard or disparaging thoughts, words, or actions.

Paul gives us a personal glimpse into his own transformation from a high-octane braggart about his Jewish ethnicity to a new man in Christ. Look carefully at what he says about his own adaptability:

> For though I am free from all, I have made myself a servant to all, that I might win more of them. To the Jews I became as a Jew, in order to win Jews. . . . To those outside the law I became as one outside the law (not being outside the law of God but under the law of Christ) that I might win those outside the law. . . . I do it all for the sake of the gospel, that I may share with them in its blessings. (1 Cor. 9:19–23)

Christians: New Race, New Ethnicity

Here's the strangest and most surprising thing about these words. Even though Paul was ethnically a Jew, he said, "To the Jews I became as a Jew." What does that mean? How can a Jew become a Jew? Does it mean he had switched ethnicities and was now a Gentile outside the law, so that he could sometimes "become" a Jew? No. Because he also said, "To those outside the law I became as one outside the law." Well, who was he?

He was a Christian. He was a new creation in Christ— a new kind of human being. "If anyone is in Christ, he is a new creation. The old has passed away; behold, the new has come" (2 Cor. 5:17). The calling of this kind of person—this new creation—is "to put on the new self, created after the likeness of God in true righteousness and holiness" (Eph. 4:24). Christ died to "create in himself *one new man*" (Eph. 2:15).

The more you think about these words in a world like ours— I mean a global world like ours—the more astonishing, radical, and revolutionary they become. Almost every country and every region of our world is torn by racial and ethnic tension, or outright violence. It is a global and contemporary problem— in many places a problem of deep and deadly proportions.

Without Paul, I Would Not Be Who I Am

No follower of Jesus has said more important or more explosive things about race and ethnicity than the apostle Paul. My world was blown up by this man. And I love him for it. I shudder to think of what I could still be apart from Paul's radical call to a new humanity in Christ. I wouldn't have preached the way I preach. I wouldn't have lived where I live. I wouldn't have the friends I have. I wouldn't have written the books I have written. I wouldn't have the same hopes for the church and for heaven that I have. And I wouldn't have an African American daughter. I would be impoverished spiritually and relationally.

At times I feel that I have scarcely begun to see the glories of Christ in the cross and what God achieved by it. But I have seen something. I have tasted enough of God's glorious aim for the age to come to know some of what it might look like here. Here's a picture of the future that the blood of Christ purchased:

> Worthy are you [Lord Jesus] to take the scroll
>   and to open its seals,
> for you were slain, and *by your blood* you ransomed
>   people for God
>   *from every tribe and language and people and nation,*
> and you have made them a *kingdom* and *priests* to
>   our God,
>   and they shall *reign* on the earth. (Rev. 5:9–10)

People from every ethnicity, ransomed by the blood of Jesus. Why? So we might be priests serving the Lord together in one temple, coreigning in one kingdom with Christ. No hostility, no tension, no distrust, no disrespect, no disregard or disparaging thoughts. Only perfect love and peace and justice. I love this picture. And I love the apostle who painted it for me.

9

My Friend with the Best News during Cancer

When the doctor told me there was an irregularity and that he would like to do a biopsy—now—the Lord Jesus used Paul's words to steady me in those minutes and in the following months: "I have not destined you for wrath."

Two hours before writing this sentence, I received a phone call from a friend whose adult son was just told by the doctor that the medical professionals have done all they can do and that barring a miracle, his cancer will be fatal. This would be the second child my friend has lost to cancer. I mention this because I am painfully aware that not everyone gets a reprieve from the cancer diagnosis the way I did—so far.

There are several ironies surrounding my own experience with cancer. My biopsy for prostate cancer happened on our thirty-seventh wedding anniversary, and the surgery to remove the cancerous gland happened on Valentine's Day. It's okay if you smile, even though cancer is not a laughing matter.

A Routine Exam, and Everything Changes

To show you the role the apostle Paul played in this, let me set the stage. It was a routine checkup with my urologist, after years of dealing with the troubling effects of an enlarged prostate. I was sixty years old and, I thought, in good health. Strange, isn't it, how we presume we are in good health when, in fact, we have no idea what is growing inside of us.

When people ask me now, "How's your health?" I never say, "Fine," like I used to. I say, "I *feel* fine." Which, being translated, means, "I don't know how I am. Only God knows. For all I know, I could have fatal cancer, or an aortic aneurysm that will burst tomorrow, or a blood clot in my leg that will release tonight and cause a fatal stroke as I sleep."

Here's what changed that simple habit of saying, "Fine." My routine exam is over. But the doctor says, "I felt some irregularities. I'd like to do a biopsy." Pause. I say, "Okay, if you say so. When?" "Now," he says, "if you have time." Pause again, as this sinks in. "Sure."

He takes me to another examination room, tells me to change into the robe hanging on the hook, and says he will be back in a few minutes with the machine for the biopsy. He goes out and leaves me alone.

Paul's Perfectly Timed Gift

At this point, you remember your best friends—the ones you spend the most time with and who tell you what you most need to hear, when you need to hear it. Well, I had spent significant time early that morning with my friend the apostle Paul. In fact, I had loved his words so much that morning that I had committed two verses to memory.

As I sat there on the examination table with my legs dangling over the end, wearing my open-backed hospital gown, and waiting for I knew not what, Paul's words came back to me.

> God has not destined [you] for wrath, but to obtain salvation through our Lord Jesus Christ, who died for [you] so that whether [you] are awake or asleep [you] might live with him. (1 Thess. 5:9–10)

This was an exquisite gift to me. Perfectly timed. Perfectly expressed. *Paul* had spoken the words that morning. But *God* had arranged for me to read them during my devotions. *God* had put it in my heart to memorize them. *God* had brought them to my mind in the examination room. And *God* had given me the faith to embrace them as the sweetest gift he could give in that moment. Yes, even sweeter than "You will be healed."

No Maverick Cells outside God's Control

But Paul was his instrument. His spokesman. His emissary to my need. I knew the voice of God because I knew the voice of his ambassador. This was vintage Paul. Here's the tailor-made news he spoke to me.

First, he told me, "What you are about to experience—cancer or not—is *not* wrath! If you have cancer, it is *not* owing to God's punishment."

To feel the full force of this, you need to realize that I share Paul's unshakable conviction that God is absolutely in control of whether anyone gets cancer. Paul said, "From him and through him and to him are all things. To him be glory forever.

Amen" (Rom. 11:36). He said, "[He] works all things according to the counsel of his will" (Eph. 1:11).

So when Paul said to me, "This is *not* the wrath of God," he did *not* mean, "If you have cancer, it's not from God." No. No. If I have cancer (which I did), it is most certainly owing to God's ultimate purposes. God controls every molecule in the universe. He is God! There are no maverick cells outside his control.

What Paul meant when he said, "This is *not* the wrath of God," is that, cancer or not, "God is *not* punishing you." This is not punitive. God has his purposes, but they do not include punishment for my sin. They are all mercy. All love. How do I know that? Paul answers that question. I will come back to it in number 4 below.

Better than No Death

Second, Paul told me, as I waited for the doctor, the positive side of "This is not wrath." He said, "God has not destined [you] for wrath, but *to obtain salvation.*"

This cancer is not wrath. It is the path to salvation. Salvation is the positive counterpart to no wrath. Did he mean, "The biopsy will come back cancer-free. You will be *saved* from having cancer"? No. That is not what he meant.

There is no question about this. Paul said, in effect, that I might die from the cancer they are about to detect. So what, then, does salvation consist in? He will get to that.

Third, Paul told me that God does not guarantee I will escape death from this cancer.

He said that I would be saved "whether [you] are awake or asleep." This means "whether you live or die." Paul called death *sleep* not because after death there is no conscious fellowship with Jesus (Phil. 1:23), but because the body of a dead

Christian looks like it is sleeping, and that body will be raised from the dead (as from sleep) at the last day (1 Cor. 15:20).

You might think this would be small comfort—not being told that I was going to survive this cancer. But that is not the way it worked. What I needed at that moment was a comfort far more solid and lasting and unshakable than a few more years of life after cancer. I needed just what I got: "This is not wrath. You are destined for salvation. And that is true—absolutely true—whether you live or die!"

Of First Importance: Christ Died for Our Sins

Fourth, Paul gave the awesome answer to the question: "How do you know this cancer is not the punishment of God for your sins?" His answer is: because Christ already died for my sins. Cancer or no cancer, death or life, Paul told me that I was going to "obtain salvation *through our Lord Jesus Christ, who died for [you]*."

At moments like these, we realize why Paul said, "I delivered to you *as of first importance* . . . that Christ died for our sins in accordance with the Scriptures, that he was buried, that he was raised on the third day in accordance with the Scriptures" (1 Cor. 15:3–4). "Of first importance" is that "Christ died for our sins." Why?

Because if he died for them, we will not die for them. That would be double jeopardy. That was the reason he came—that Jesus might endure my condemnation under the wrath of God by dying on the cross (John 3:36; Rom. 8:3). The person who is united to Christ by faith in him "does not come into judgment, but has passed from death to life" (John 5:24).

That's why Paul said, "There is therefore now no condemnation for those who are in Christ Jesus" (Rom. 8:1). No condemnation because Christ bore the condemnation. No wrath because Christ bore the wrath. That's why Paul said to me so clearly and firmly and joyfully, as I waited for the biopsy, "This cancer is *not* wrath."

Paul's Gift Was the Promise of a Person

The final thing he said to me was very personal, namely, just what he meant by *salvation*. "God has not destined [you] for wrath, but to obtain salvation through our Lord Jesus Christ, who died for [you] so that whether [you] are awake or asleep *[you] might live with him*."

Whether you live or die, you will live. But not just live in some misty, unspecified immortality, but very specifically, "you will live *with him*"—the One who died for you and rose again. Which means at least two great things. One is that I will live *forever*, since the One I live with cannot die. "Christ, being raised from the dead, will never die again" (Rom. 6:9). The other is that I get to live forever with the One who loved me enough to die for me. This is a very personal and deeply satisfying promise.

The doctor called me the next day and said, "You have cancer. I'd like to meet with you and your wife when it's convenient for you and discuss your options." We took the radical option: take it out. That happened seven weeks later—on Valentine's Day. That was twelve years ago. How am I doing? I feel fine.

One More Happy Surprise from Paul's Logic: a Helmet

Paul had one more surprise for me. Only later did I notice the significance of the fact that his words to me that morning began with *for*.

> *For* God has not destined [you] for wrath, but to obtain salvation through our Lord Jesus Christ, who died for [you] so that whether [you] are awake or asleep [you] might live with him. (1 Thess. 5:9–10)

This means that the promise he gave me was the ground or the basis for what he had just said. Namely, "For a helmet [put on] the hope of salvation" (v. 8). In other words, the promise Paul gave me that morning was the basis of my hope, and that hope was like a helmet.

This simply added a new layer of understanding and thankfulness for what Paul and the Lord Jesus had done for me that day in the urologist's office. Think of it. What were helmets for? They were for protection in mortal battle. A blow to the head with a mace or a bludgeon would crush your skull and kill you. So can the news of cancer.

Without my even thinking in those terms, the Lord Jesus took Paul's promise in 1 Thessalonians 5:9–10 and put it on my head like a helmet. He protected me first from the biopsy blow, and then from the cancer blow, with this helmet. God covered my head with the promise that these blows were not wrath. He positioned the helmet of hope perfectly without my even thinking of helmets. I simply thought, *This is not wrath; and if I live, I live with Christ, and if I die, I also live with Christ.* With that he covered my head.

Paul is not the only writer in the Bible who has covered my head with promises in the hour of trial. But this trial was memorable and intense. When you walk through such trials with a friend like this, God builds an unusual bond of love.

10

Learning Late in Life to Know and Kill My Most Besetting Sins

Under Christ, no one has humbled me, diagnosed me, exposed me, taught me, and empowered me to make war on my besetting sins the way Paul has. I think I owe him the survival and flourishing of my ministry and my marriage.

When I was sixty-four years old, I took an eight-month leave of absence from my pastoral ministry. The primary reason I gave to the leaders and to the congregation was that I wanted to step back and do a soul check.

I wondered if the pressures of ministry might be blinding me to the state of my own soul as it related to worship and family and marriage and personal holiness. There was no great marriage crisis. I was not walking in any ministry-disqualifying sin, as far as I knew myself. But the stresses of family and marriage and ministry were enough to make me think that I should temporarily remove the pressure (and rewards) of preaching, and leading the staff, and all writing and social media.

During those eight months, my wife and I attended another church and simply participated as part of the worshiping congregation. Part of my goal was to check my soul and see whether I could authentically, joyfully engage in public worship without being the leader or the preacher. I wanted to make sure that I was not confusing the adrenaline surge of up-front leadership and preaching with authentic, personal joy in Jesus himself alongside other believers.

Putting the Crosshairs on Besetting Sins

Another goal was to have the time and emotional energy and relational engagement with my wife so as to be as penetrating as I could be in identifying and addressing my most besetting sins, especially as they related to our relationship.

During those eight months, no one walked with me more closely or helpfully than the apostle Paul. I don't say this to minimize the grace of the overseeing elders or the patience and involvement of my wife. I say it to pay tribute to the enormity of the mercy I received from the Lord Jesus through the revelation of indispensable truth for fighting sin that came through the apostle Paul.

As always, Paul was not the only biblical spokesman who came alongside me. But without a doubt, he was the most penetrating and the most powerful. This is true of the diagnosis and the treatment of my besetting sins. What follows is a very abbreviated summary of what happened.

Naming the Sins

As I tried to be very specific in identifying my characteristic sins, it became evident what they were—namely, an ugly cluster of selfishness, anger, self-pity, quickness to blame, and sullenness. If you wonder whether, in not mentioning sex, I am trying to conceal some secret struggle with sexual lust, all I can say is that the measure of victory I enjoyed (and still enjoy) over that sin is far greater than over this destructive constellation of sins. And I am sure that my wife would testify that sexual temptation does not threaten to unravel the beautiful fabric of our marriage like these sins do. Of course, let him who thinks that he stands take heed lest he fall (1 Cor. 10:12).

Under Paul's Spirit-given searchlight, I was led not only to identify these five sins but also to be ruthlessly specific in describing them. What follows first here is a description of my understanding and experience of selfishness.

What Is My Selfishness?

Selfishness is virtually the same as pride and is at the heart of what Paul calls *indwelling sin* (Rom. 7:23)—sin that remains in me as a believer. It is the corruption of my heart that is at the bottom of all my sinning. I see my selfishness function as a reflex in these five ways:

- I expect to be served.
- I feel that I am owed.
- I want praise.
- I expect that things will go my way.
- I feel that I have the right to react negatively to being crossed.

The reason I use the word *reflex* to describe these traits of selfishness is that there is zero premeditation before they happen. When these responses happen, they are coming from my fallen nature, not from reflection and resolution. I don't sin out of duty. I sin spontaneously. They are the reflexes of my original, unmortified sinfulness.

Specific Sinful Effects of Selfishness

Now, what happens inside of me when this selfishness is crossed? Can I name these effects and describe them specifically? Vague generalizations are usually evasions. Paul was teaching me that I must be specific. Here are the four effects of my selfishness being crossed.

- *Anger*: the strong emotional opposition to the obstacle in my way. I tighten up and want to strike out verbally.

- *Self-pity*: a desire that others feel my woundedness and admire me for my being mistreated, and move to show me some sympathy.

- *Quickness to blame*: a reflex to attribute to others the cause of my frustrating situation. Others can feel it in a tone of voice, a look on the face, a sideways query, or an outright accusation.

- *Sullenness*: a sinking discouragement, moodiness, hopelessness, unresponsiveness, and withdrawn emotional deadness.

And, of course, the effect on marriage is that my wife feels blamed and disapproved of rather than cherished and cared for. Tender emotions shrivel. Hope is depleted. Strength to carry on in the hardships of ministry wanes. And worst of all, these sins, as Paul makes clear, are "not in step with the truth of the gospel" (Gal. 2:14)—not "worthy of the gospel" (Phil. 1:27).

Paul Reveals an Inconsistency

During these months of self-assessment, Paul made crystal clear for me the connection between Christ's cancellation of my sins on the cross and my conscious, willed conquering of my sins through blood-bought, Spirit-empowered effort. In other words, he blasted the pattern of passivity that I had developed in relation to these sins. He forced into my face the biblical reality that canceled sins must be killed, not coddled.

He showed me, for example, an important inconsistency I was living in. On the one hand, I believed in, and acted on, the necessity of my conscious effort in killing sexual lust. But I was more passive when it came to these ugly effects of selfishness. I had the unspoken assumption that lust must be attacked directly and consciously, since Jesus said to tear out your eye if you have to (Matt. 5:29). But for some reason, I assumed that I could not attack these besetting sins in the same way. They had to somehow dry up and disappear by an inner, unconscious work of the Spirit, without my effort.

The Only Sins We Can Defeat Are Forgiven Sins

Don't get me wrong. Paul made it clear that Christ's death for my sins preceded and enabled my defeating my sins. Here are the big words for this: my justification precedes my sanctification. Being *counted righteous* in Christ precedes *becoming righteous* in behavior. When we sing, "He breaks the power of canceled sin" in the hymn "O for a Thousand Tongues to Sing," we are getting the order exactly right. First, our sin is *canceled* by the death of Christ (Col. 2:14). And only then can we *break its power* by the Spirit.

But it became increasingly clear during these eight months that the link between the cancellation of my sin on the cross and the conquering of my sin was sanctified effort. To be sure, the only effort that avails is blood-bought, Spirit-wrought effort. But it is, nevertheless, a conscious effort of my will. Passivity in the pursuit of holiness is not what Paul teaches. Paul piles up illustrations of how this works. I look back now and wonder: How had I become so passive?

Three of Paul's Pictures

Here are three of Paul's pictures of how the death of Christ cancels my sin and leads to effort.

1. In the death of Christ, *we died* to sin. "We have been united with him in a death like his" (Rom. 6:5). Therefore, actively put sin to death. "You also must consider yourselves dead to sin" (Rom. 6:11). "Let not sin therefore reign in your mortal body" (Rom. 6:12).

2. In the death of Christ, *we were bought*. "You are not your own, for you were bought with a price" (1 Cor. 6:19–20). Therefore, actively glorify your new owner. "Glorify God in your body" (1 Cor. 6:20).

3. In the death of Christ, *we were forgiven*. "God in Christ forgave you" (Eph. 4:32). Therefore, forgive. "Be kind to one another, tenderhearted, forgiving one another" (Eph. 4:32).

In every case, *the decisive impulse* for my active effort in pursuing holiness—my active sin-killing—is the death of Christ. This means that the decisive power for *conquering* my besetting sins comes from the reality that Christ already *canceled* them. The only sins that I can defeat are forgiven sins.

"Tear Out Your Eye" Applies to More than Lust

But here's what I had been missing: in each of these three cases, the link between the cross and my conquered sin is *my empowered will*. I say that because, in each of these three cases, Paul makes the statement of my *death*, my *purchase*, and my *forgiveness* the cause of a *command* addressed to my will. "Let not sin . . . reign in your mortal body." "Glorify God in your body." "Be kind to one another, tenderhearted, forgiving one another." Those commands are addressed to me. They engage my will.

In other words, God intends that part of my experience of sanctification be conscious, willed opposition to specific sins in my life. I had applied that to lust. But for some reason, I had failed to apply the same brutal intentionality of sin killing to my selfishness, anger, self-pity, quickness to blame, and sullenness.

Do! For God Is Doing

At this point Paul took hold of me and rubbed my nose in Philippians 2:12–13:

> Therefore, my beloved, as you have always obeyed, so now, not only as in my presence but much more in my absence, work out your own salvation with fear and trembling, for it is God who works in you, both to will and to work for his good pleasure.

I saw two things in a fresh light:

> 1. I saw afresh that the verb "*work out* your salvation" (Greek *katergazesthe*) means *produce*, or *bring about*, or *effect*. In his Philippians commentary, Peter O'Brien sums it up with the phrase "continuous, sustained, strenuous effort."[1] Of course, this language is dangerous. It might lead some to work without depending on Christ's prior justifying work, and without depending on the Spirit. But Paul doesn't make that mistake. He presupposes here the cross and the Spirit. Then he says: Now stop being passive! Not all sin dies of itself. Some must be actively killed.

---

1. Peter T. O'Brien, *The Epistle to the Philippians*, New International Greek Testament Commentary (Grand Rapids, MI: 1991), 279.

2. I saw afresh that the salvation I was to work out was not only the large reality of total deliverance, but also the concrete reality of deliverance from selfishness, anger, self-pity, blaming, and sullenness.

What It Looks Like in Practice

The overall effect of these discoveries was a new and focused attack on specific sins, with a kind of intentionality I had never exercised before, except in fighting sexual lust. When I came back to the church from this eight-month leave, I spoke about all this in the Bethlehem College & Seminary chapel and used the following illustration to help them understand what I was learning.

On a recent Sunday evening, it was cozy and snowy, and my wife and daughter and I were home alone. I was looking forward to something we would all do together. But my fourteen-year-old daughter came in from the dining room and said, "Mommy and I are going to watch *Supernanny* on the computer." They set it up and started watching—without me.

Now, as insignificant as this incident seems, in that moment the temptation for selfishness, anger, self-pity, blaming, and sullenness were as dangerous to my soul as any sexual temptation. So, with new intentionality and ruthlessness, I immediately said to those rising sinful feelings, *No!*—not out loud, but to my sinful soul. Then I quietly went upstairs, consciously renouncing any body language of woundedness (though I was feeling it).

In my study, I waged war. Effort! I turned my mind and heart toward the promises of God, and the surety of the cross, and the love of the Father, and the wealth of my inheritance in Christ, and the blessings of that Lord's Day, and the patience of Jesus. And I held them there in my mind where I could see them.

I cried to the Lord for blood-bought help, and I consciously, intentionally (not passively!) beat down the anger and self-pity and blaming and sullenness, as utterly out of character with who I am in Jesus Christ (1 Cor. 5:7). And I kept beating until they were effectively dead.

Good Growth Now, Better Days Ahead

I freely admit that it would be far better—a sign of greater maturity and sanctification—if there did not have to be any war at all, if I had never felt these sinful feelings rising in my heart. That will come. But until then, I thank God that he cancels sin at the cross, that he breaks the power of canceled sin, and that he does it sometimes through my Spirit-empowered will that fights with all its might.

And I thank God for Paul. Under Christ, no one humbled me, diagnosed me, exposed me, taught me, and delivered me the way he did. How can you not love a comrade in arms, a marriage counselor, and a ministry saver like this man!

PART 3

A MIND FOR LOGIC, A HEART FOR LOVE

11

Rigorous in Reasoning, Transparent in Feeling

Paul's soul was marked by the beautiful interweaving of enormous powers of reason and profound capacities for emotion, both of which he put in the service of others.

Virtually all who have undertaken, with patience and rigor, to trace Paul's thinking in his letter to the Romans agree: here is a towering intellect at work. Some have called Romans the greatest letter ever written, if only for the majesty of its content and the meticulousness of its reasoning. Even his enemies saw these intellectual gifts:

> As [Paul] was saying these things in his defense, Festus [the Roman governor] said with a loud voice, "Paul, you are out of your mind; your great learning is driving you out of your mind." (Acts 26:24)

"In Your Thinking Be Mature"

Paul believed that the serious application of mental power is part of what it means to follow Christ. Though formally educated at the feet of a famous teacher (Acts 22:3), Paul did not see himself as the kind of intellectual who would use his powers to outwit others and exalt himself. He did not want his converts to be mindless. He called all Christians to think for themselves:

> Brothers, do not be children in your thinking. Be infants in evil, but *in your thinking be mature*. (1 Cor. 14:20)

> *Think over what I say*, for the Lord will give you understanding in everything. (2 Tim. 2:7)

> I speak as to sensible people; *judge for yourselves* what I say. (1 Cor. 10:15)

Even the apostle Peter, in his second letter, drew attention to the complexity and difficulty involved in understanding some of what Paul wrote:

> There are some things in [his letters] that are hard to understand, which the ignorant and unstable twist to their own destruction, as they do the other Scriptures. (2 Pet. 3:16)

Emotionally Tender and Transparent

But in spite of the complexity and profundity of his reasoning, the emotional maturity and full humanity of the man shine through the depth and tenderness and intensity of his emotions, which (like his own imperfections) he was willing to reveal.

> We were *gentle* among you, like a nursing mother taking care of her own children. So, being *affectionately desirous*

of you, we were ready to share with you not only the gospel of God but also our own selves, because you had become very dear to us. (1 Thess. 2:7–8)

My brothers, whom *I love and long for*, my joy and crown, stand firm thus in the Lord, my *beloved*. (Phil. 4:1)

God is my witness, how *I yearn for you all with the affection* of Christ Jesus. (Phil. 1:8)

I am sending [Onesimus] back to you, sending *my very heart*. (Philem. 12)

We have spoken freely to you, Corinthians; *our heart is wide open*. You are not restricted by us, but you are restricted in your own affections. In return (I speak as to children) widen your hearts also. (2 Cor. 6:11–13)

Rare Combination of Mind and Heart

Many people in this world are lopsidedly rational and struggle to express real emotion. And many other people are very emotional and have a hard time following a complex argument, let alone constructing one. Few are the people who have extraordinary powers of reason and at the same time have tender hearts and a facility for expressing emotion that brings encouragement and joy to others.

As I meet Paul in his letters, he stands out as one of those rare people. This is significant. His combination of rationality and emotional authenticity are not the mark of a deluded or deceptive man. He bears the marks of a mature, mentally healthy, and stable man. His powers of intellect may have threatened some. But his empathy and his capacities for compassion and tender affection take away our intimidation and win our hearts. At least, *my* mind is wakened and *my* heart is won.

12

Speaking with Feeling about the Glory of Christ, Not Religious Activity

Even though Paul could have boasted in his superior achievements above most in his generation, and even though his rank and accomplishments in the church were as high as you can go, he nevertheless preferred to exult in and speak of the preciousness of personally knowing Jesus.

My admiration is drawn to people whose achievements are remarkable but who cherish Jesus over the recognition that comes from great accomplishments. So many Christians seem to speak readily about church growth, ministry experiences, ethical issues in society, crises of persecution, the state of our youth, the current musical trend, and more, but they do not readily speak of the preciousness of their fellowship with Jesus.

Something feels dysfunctional about this kind of Christianity—as if the essence of spiritual reality were found in deeds rather than the relationship with the divine person who inspires and shapes and sustains those deeds. It's as if what is really interesting and captivating is the shape of the shell, not the taste of the nut. It is sad that so many Christians have such an easy time talking about religious activity but such a hard time talking about spiritual taste. Not the apostle Paul.

Great Achievements before and after Conversion

Paul was at the top of his religious game when Jesus knocked him off his horse. And even after his conversion, he was among the most authoritative and productive Christians of his day. He had lots of "religious activity" he could talk about. His old religious cronies tried to put him in the shade by boasting of their religious rigors. Paul could have beat them at their game. In fact, several times Paul reached back into his astonishing religious résumé and silenced his naysayers with words like these:

> If anyone else thinks he has reason for confidence in the flesh, I have more: circumcised on the eighth day, of the people of Israel, of the tribe of Benjamin, a Hebrew of Hebrews; as to the law, a Pharisee; as to zeal, a persecutor of the church; as to righteousness under the law, blameless. (Phil. 3:4–7)

> I was advancing in Judaism beyond many of my own age among my people, so extremely zealous was I for the traditions of my fathers. (Gal. 1:14)

Even after he became a Christian, his achievements were unsurpassed. Now and then, he referred to his hard work and spiritual authority and fruitfulness. But every time he did that, he confessed his utter dependence on the grace of God. He wanted to glory in Christ himself, not in his own hard work, or his miracles, or his visions.

> By the grace of God I am what I am, and his grace toward me was not in vain. On the contrary, I worked harder than any of them, though it was not I, but the grace of God that is with me. (1 Cor. 15:10)

> I was not at all inferior to these super-apostles, even though I am nothing. (2 Cor. 12:11)

> What then is Apollos? What is Paul? Servants through whom you believed, as the Lord assigned to each. I planted, Apollos watered, but God gave the growth. So neither he who plants nor he who waters is anything, but only God who gives the growth. (1 Cor. 3:5–7)

Jesus Was His Joy, Explicitly

Paul's achievements were superior before he became a Christian and after he became a Christian. But they were not his glory. They were not his joy. He showed where his glory and joy lay most clearly when he compared his enjoyment of Christ with his enjoyment of his achievements.

> Whatever gain I had, I counted as loss for the sake of Christ. Indeed, I count everything as loss because of the surpassing worth of knowing Christ Jesus my Lord. For his sake I have suffered the loss of all things and count them as rubbish, in order that I may gain Christ. (Phil. 3:7–8)

Jesus himself—knowing him in all his inestimable worth—was his highest glory and joy. Achievements were secondary. Jesus himself, known and enjoyed, was primary. Paul had a vibrant sense of being loved by Jesus in a way that touched him every day. He described his life like this:

I have been crucified with Christ. It is no longer I who live, but Christ who lives in me. And the life I now live in the flesh I live by faith in the Son of God, *who loved me and gave himself for me.* (Gal. 2:20)

Paul was so united to Christ—Christ's love for him and his faith in Christ—that there was a profound sense in which Christ was living out his life through Paul. This was Paul's delight. This was the heart of his boasting and exultation. We would not have conversed with him long before hearing him share this great love of his.

A Very Special Friend

I long for this attitude in the people I relate to. I long for this kind of communication—the kind that moves through achievements to personal fellowship with the risen Christ. That's why, when I see it so beautifully in Paul, I feel I have found a very special friend.

From Logic on Fire
to Lyrics of Love

Not only could Paul think and write at the most demanding intellectual level, but he also could write poetically, beautifully, and with such universal appeal that some of his words are among the most widely quoted in the world, even by non-Christians.

I realize that this is no great moral achievement—to write so compellingly. Even bad people have written demanding essays, beautiful prose, and arresting poetry. So what's the point of including such an observation—his writing gift—among the reasons that I love the apostle Paul?

A Bright Blue Brushstroke on the Canvas of His Life

Well, every brushstroke in a beautiful painting does not have to be amazing in and of itself. Many aren't. A single brushstroke may just add a touch that, together with all the others, makes the whole painting more attractive. It's as though you get to know someone, find out dozens of beautiful things about him, grow to trust him implicitly, and then discover: *Are you kidding me? On top of everything else, he's a craftsman! A poet!*

That's the way this works for me. It's a brushstroke of bright blue that may seem superfluous but makes me smile with joy that it belongs to this portrait of Paul.

From Logic to Lyrics

Paul has the reputation of writing in long, logically intricate sentences that develop extended, involved arguments. For example, verses 3–14 of Ephesians 1 are one long sentence! Most people who study Paul would say that his letter to the Romans is a spectacular example of careful argumentation. He writes with logical precision and careful attention to clarity and cogency.

Therefore, when we come to chapter 13 of 1 Corinthians, we are surprised. The chapter comes right in the middle of a very controversial discussion of spiritual gifts. On either side of chapter 13 are chapters that deal with this contentious issue. Sandwiched in between comes what most people who know Paul would say is the most beautiful passage he ever wrote— beautiful in the combination of *morally* luminous thought combined with *aesthetically* arresting prose. Some would say *poetry*. It might help to quote the whole thing:

> If I speak in the tongues of men and of angels, but have not love, I am a noisy gong or a clanging cymbal. And if I have prophetic powers, and understand all mysteries and all knowledge, and if I have all faith, so as to remove mountains, but have not love, I am nothing. If I give away all I have, and if I deliver up my body to be burned, but have not love, I gain nothing.

Love is patient and kind; love does not envy or boast; it is not arrogant or rude. It does not insist on its own way; it is not irritable or resentful; it does not rejoice at wrong-doing, but rejoices with the truth. Love bears all things, believes all things, hopes all things, endures all things.

Love never ends. As for prophecies, they will pass away; as for tongues, they will cease; as for knowledge, it will pass away. For we know in part and we prophesy in part, but when the perfect comes, the partial will pass away. When I was a child, I spoke like a child, I thought like a child, I reasoned like a child. When I became a man, I gave up childish ways. For now we see in a mirror dimly, but then face to face. Now I know in part; then I shall know fully, even as I have been fully known. So now faith, hope, and love abide, these three; but the greatest of these is love.

This chapter is beautiful in its pithiness, cadences, imagery, development, crescendo, theme, and completeness. This is unlike anything else Paul wrote. But the attempt to say he didn't write it, but borrowed it, shatters on one other beauty: the controversy of chapters 12 and 14 are woven into chapter 13. This chapter is not a meteor that landed in the middle of a controversy, with little connection to its surroundings. It is a tapestry woven out of threads taken from the controversy. This is not secondhand.

That Paul could rise to this kind of poetic achievement in the midst of a controversial discussion is extraordinary. His stylistic repertoire is not as limited as we might have thought. His capabilities as a writer are not narrow. He is gifted in more ways than we may have realized.

The Moral Dimension of Paul's Prose

This brings me back to the thought that this ability in writing is no great moral achievement. The longer I stare at this bright brushstroke in the portrait of Paul's greatness, the less sure of that I become. On the one hand, writing the way he usually writes—developing precise arguments with cogency and clarity—is not, in my view, morally neutral. It is a sign of honesty. To give reasons for what you believe and to strive for clarity that reveals what you truly think are marks of integrity.

What then about the moral dimension of the depth and beauty of this greatest of all chapters on love? Where did this come from? Was it merely the morally neutral function of natural skill? It strikes me that someone with these outstanding logical and poetic gifts could have made a great name for himself in the literary world of Roman and Jewish culture. But instead, Paul followed the path of suffering as an apostle of Christ. He subordinated great possibilities as a celebrity to the service of Christ's church. This, in itself, adds another beauty to 1 Corinthians 13—that it is not published in a literary journal but woven into a letter humbly trying to help ordinary people love each other.

In fact, when I consider how Paul chose a path of suffering instead of a literary career, I can't help but wonder whether 1 Corinthians 13 really could have been written without this suffering. Perhaps, then, this bright blue brushstroke is not so incidental to the moral beauty of Paul's life. Perhaps it belongs not to the periphery, but to the center of why I love him.

14

Turning High Thoughts to the Help of the Lowly

Though Paul could deal in the "unsearchable riches of Christ," his burden was to awaken and sustain in all Christians "a sincere and pure devotion to Christ." So he "behaved in the world with simplicity and godly sincerity, not by earthly wisdom but by the grace of God."

On the one hand, it is admirable to have insight into profound truth, but not if it puffs you up and makes you indifferent to the needs that ordinary people have, such as the need for truth that they can understand and put to practical use for their temporal and eternal good. On the other hand, it is admirable to be practical and understandable and down to earth, but not if it comes with a kind of reverse snobbery that shuns complex realities and measures truth and value by a purely pragmatic standard.

Profound and Practical

Paul was profound and practical. Or, to say it another way, he loved God and people. His love for God summoned him ever higher into God's revealed glory. His love for people summoned him alongside ordinary folks with explanations and encouragements that helped them grow from where they were to new levels of wisdom and goodness and joy.

Paul was given insight into great mysteries, which he called the "unsearchable riches of Christ" (Eph. 3:8; cf. Col. 1:27). He could lead his readers so far up into these mysteries that when he came down he would say, "How unsearchable are his judgments and how inscrutable his ways!" (Rom. 11:33).

All my admiration for Paul's soaring spiritual insight and wisdom would vanish if he looked with scorn on ordinary people and used his apostolic wisdom and his natural intellect to win applause, rather than to communicate in a way that built up their faith. But Paul was intensely vigilant against this danger.

Let Everything Be Done for Upbuilding, Even by Big Shots

When Paul was dealing with the Corinthian Christians' unloving use of their spiritual gifts, he emphasized that everything should be done to build others up. They were speaking in tongues without any interpretation, so no one was understanding and no one's faith was being built up. So Paul said, "Let all things be done for building up" (1 Cor. 14:26). Then he practiced what he preached:

> You may be giving thanks well enough, but the other person is not being built up. I thank God that I speak in tongues more than all of you. Nevertheless, in church I would rather speak five words with my mind in order to instruct others, than ten thousand words in a tongue. (1 Cor. 14:17–19)

This is astonishing. If anyone could boast in the unusual, supernatural gift of speaking in tongues, Paul says he could. But Paul did not want to advance his own reputation of spiritual superiority. He wanted to help ordinary people understand truth and grow in their faith.

Simplicity and Godly Sincerity

When the Corinthians' faith was in jeopardy, he was deeply concerned: "I am afraid that as the serpent deceived Eve by his cunning, your thoughts will be led astray from a sincere and pure devotion to Christ" (2 Cor. 11:3). This is what he was after: "sincere and pure devotion to Christ." How could he help that come about? Not by ignoring the "unsearchable riches of Christ." Not by marginalizing glorious reality. How then? Like this:

> We behaved in the world with simplicity and godly sincerity, not by earthly wisdom but by the grace of God, and supremely so toward you. For we are not writing to you anything other than what you read and understand and I hope you will fully understand. (2 Cor. 1:12–13)

Paul could soar into the theological heights with the greatest prophets and philosophers. He was that gifted, and that inspired. And yet he did not give way to any proud desire to lord it over his people. He did not flaunt his capacities to soar. Instead, he acted "with simplicity and godly sincerity." He aimed to be understood by ordinary people. It is beautiful when a great mind loves like this. It wins my trust and admiration.

PART 4

MAKING THE
MYSTERIES SING

15

More Awed by the Glory Revealed than the Glory Concealed

Though Paul confessed that the ways of God are inscrutable, and his judgments unsearchable, he does not stay in the lowlands of divine revelation but leads us up into heights of God's ways and judgments, so that when we put our hands over our mouths, it is because we are amazed not at the Appalachians but at the Alps—not at God's arithmetic, but at his calculus.

I have read writers and heard speakers who try to turn our ignorance about God's ways into the main ground for our amazement and worship. They usually do so by using the positive word *mystery* to refer to the depths and heights of God so that we are supposed to be moved with wonder and awe at how much we do not know about God.

This has always seemed misleading to me. I'm not drawn to people who do this. Paul's approach is very different. He would say that God is most glorified when we are stunned and admiring and worshipful and joyfully submitted to him because of what we *do* know about him, not because of what we *don't* know about him.

Your admiration and wonder at a mountain range might be based on your glimpse from the foothills, where you see the range rise and disappear into low-lying clouds. Or it might be based on years of expeditions into the mountain range only to discover that every time you reach the top of one unimaginably high peak, another entire range of mountains soars before you and above you.

It is no great honor to God to spend your life in the foothills, writing essays and poems about how much you don't know above the cloud line. Far better to let God put your hand into the hand of Paul, and then spend a lifetime climbing with him on the high paths of revelation.

"Unsearchable and Inscrutable"?

One of the most misunderstood and misused passages in Paul's writings is the great climactic section at the end of Romans 1–11:

> Oh, the depth of the riches and wisdom and knowledge of God! How unsearchable are his judgments and how inscrutable his ways! "For who has known the mind of the Lord, or who has been his counselor?" "Or who has given a gift to him that he might be repaid?" For from him and through him and to him are all things. To him be glory forever. Amen. (Rom. 11:33–36)

Here's the key observation: Paul does not write this soaring admiration of God's riches *instead of* revealing those riches, but *because* he had just laid out those riches in eleven chapters of mind-boggling revelation. He soars because of what he had just *unveiled*, not because of all that remained *veiled*. These words of amazement come at the end of eleven chapters in which Paul has taken us into the depths and heights of God's ways beyond what any of us thought possible.

Just reading the preceding three *verses* boggles the mind about God's ways. Not because they are behind a cloud of unknowing, but because they are revealed as utterly unexpected and counterintuitive and shocking and God-exalting. Paul sums up God's plans for Jews and Gentiles:

> For just as you [Gentiles] were at one time disobedient to God but now have received mercy because of their [Jewish] disobedience, so they too have now been disobedient in order that by the mercy shown to you they also may now receive mercy. For God has consigned all to disobedience, that he may have mercy on all. (Rom. 11:30–32)

Take five minutes to reflect on those verses, and you come away at first dazed, and then amazed, not because you are left in the dark, but because the light is so dazzling you can scarcely believe what you are seeing.

"Unsearchable" but Brought to Light

Paul describes his revelation of God's ways as *unsearchable* one other time. And the point is *not* that he leaves us in the foothills without knowledge.

> To me, though I am the very least of all the saints, this grace was given, to preach to the Gentiles the *unsearchable riches of Christ*, and to *bring to light for everyone what is the plan of the mystery* hidden for ages in God, who created all things. (Eph. 3:8–9)

This text does *not* mean, "Sorry, folks, the riches of Christ are in the darkness of mystery, and they can't be revealed." The text says the opposite: "God called me," Paul says, "and gifted me to bring the mystery to light! The things I write about Christ *are* the unsearchable riches of Christ!"

They are unsearchable in three senses: (1) They have been "hidden for ages in God"—but no more! (2) They can be known only by divine revelation, not mere human wisdom—and Paul is writing that revelation. (3) There will always be more to see as you climb into the meaning of inspired revelation, and then into the Himalayas of heaven.

To Know What Surpasses Knowledge

This last point is confirmed in Paul's prayer in the next chapter of Ephesians. He prays that we

> may have strength to comprehend with all the saints what is the breadth and length and height and depth, and *to know the love of Christ that surpasses knowledge*, that you may be filled with all the fullness of God. (Eph. 3:18–19)

This is it! Because of God's stunning revelation of his ways in Christ—through the writings of the apostle Paul—we are granted "to know the love of Christ that surpasses knowledge." We are taken higher and higher into the mountain ranges of God's wonders so that we really know what was unknowable, only to find that the mountains rise ever higher.

A Sure-Footed Sherpa in the Himalayas of God's Word

I would not be writing this book if Paul were one of those people who is content to live in the foothills of revelation, waxing eloquent about the value of "mystery" above the low-lying clouds. Paul is not one of them. Paul knew that God gave him a calling not to *hide*, but to *preach* "the unsearchable riches of Christ."

Paul knows that God is honored not when we linger in the valley, endlessly extolling the value of unexplored mystery, but when we accept his invitation to lead us into his unsearchable judgments and inscrutable ways. I have found Paul to be a sure-footed Sherpa in the Himalayas of God's revelation. He has walked me through some very treacherous paths. I love him for it.

16

Reveling in God's Power
in and through Ours

Paul combined a passion for God's pervasive, providential rule over the whole world with a deep commitment to human action and responsibility.

Thinking seriously about the sheer reality of God raises questions about the extent of his power and the reality of human freedom. Of course, if you don't believe in God, you have the same kinds of questions, only they are not as personal. If there is no intelligent being behind the cosmos, then the question is not whether God governs the will of man, but whether the will of man has any meaning beyond the mere movements of molecules.

Absolute, Trinitarian Reality—God

But Paul believes in God and that all things are "from him and through him and to him" (Rom. 11:36). He believes that God has from all eternity existed as the Trinity—Father, Son, and Holy Spirit. These three are one God—one divine essence, but three persons. The Trinity may be a great mystery, but it is inescapable from what Paul teaches in his letters.

God the Son is the very image of God (2 Cor. 4:4; Col. 1:15). "In him all the fullness of God was pleased to dwell. . . . In him the whole fullness of deity dwells bodily" (Col. 1:19; 2:9). God the Spirit is the Spirit of God and the Spirit of Christ (Rom. 8:9). Through the Son all things were created and all things hold together.

> By [the Son] all things were created, in heaven and on earth.
> . . . All things were created through him and for him. And
> he is before all things, and in him all things hold together.
> (Col. 1:16–17)

So, in Paul's understanding, the universe is created and held in being by a personal God. There is no whiff of materialistic fatalism—as if the cosmos were an infinite expanse of nothing but matter and energy and time. For him the universe is radiant with an intelligent Person's handiwork. It is telling the glory of God (Rom. 1:20).

All Things according to His Will

The question arises, then, of how this pervasive creating and sustaining activity of God relates to human beings. We are not surprised when Paul says, "In him we have obtained an inheritance, having been predestined according to the purpose of him *who works all things according to the counsel of his will*" (Eph. 1:11).

For Paul, this sweeping sovereignty of God is the foundation of the best news in the world—namely, that in a world of relentless calamity and tragedy and pain and death, God turns all events for the good of those who love him. If he were not sovereign over all things, he could not turn all things for our good. Thus, Paul says, amazingly, "For those who love God all things work together for good, for those who are called according to his purpose" (Rom. 8:28).

God's Power Does Not Paralyze, but Impels

But what makes Paul's vision of the sovereignty of God so beautiful is that it does not contradict the reality and significance of our wills, but coheres perfectly in ways that astonish and empower us. For example, he says:

> By the grace of God I am what I am, and his grace toward me was not in vain. On the contrary, *I worked* harder than any of them, though *it was not I, but the grace of God* that is with me. (1 Cor. 15:10)

> *Work out your own salvation* with fear and trembling, for *it is God who works in you*, both to will and to work for his good pleasure. (Phil. 2:12–13)

> Thanks be to God, who *put into the heart of Titus* the same earnest care I have for you. For he not only accepted our appeal, but being himself very earnest he is going to you *of his own accord*. (2 Cor. 8:16–17)

What is so striking about this way of seeing reality is that God's decisive, sovereign rule in the world and in our lives is not a hindrance but a help in doing what he calls us to do. God's sovereignty does not make us fatalists. It does not paralyze us and make us say, "What will be will be." It does not disillusion us with the meaninglessness of an impersonal cosmos.

Instead, it empowers us to exert all *our* will and all *our* energy because we know this is how God works in the world—

through people. God's pervasive rule in the world gives us hope that nothing is meaningless. Nothing is merely random. All is part of God's infinite, and often inscrutable, wisdom.

Hence, as we saw in the last chapter, Paul comes to the end of one of his most exalted sections in the letter to the Romans and says:

> Oh, the depth of the riches and wisdom and knowledge of God! How unsearchable are his judgments and how inscrutable his ways! "For who has known the mind of the Lord, or who has been his counselor?" "Or who has given a gift to him that he might be repaid?" For from him and through him and to him are all things. To him be glory forever. Amen. (Rom. 11:33–36)

In all his soaring thoughts about the power and riches and wisdom and sovereignty of God, Paul is a person of joyful praise. He is not the frenzied rationalist who, as G. K. Chesterton said, is trying to get the heavens to fit inside his head. He is the happy servant of Christ who has been given the privilege of getting his own head a little way into the heavens. I love listening and learning. I love joining him there.

17

A Global Grasp of Suffering and a Heart of Personal Empathy

Paul was not naïve about the vastness of human misery and suffering in the world. And the explanation he gave, as he probed this mystery, was both personal in its application to individual Christians and universal in its cosmic scope of redemption.

Only rarely do we find a person who is able to speak meaningfully about suffering at the very personal level of pain and loss, and also at the cosmic level of why the whole universe is the way it is. Most people, it seems, are wired either to be a wise counselor who can apply God's goodness and power to individual need or to think globally about why the entire world is permeated, for all its beauty, with horrifying calamities. Finding both in one person is rare and beautiful. Paul was such a person.

Teaching New Believers to Suffer

Within weeks after starting a new church and appointing leaders for the church, Paul prepared the new believers to suffer.

> When they had preached the gospel . . . they returned to Lystra and to Iconium and to Antioch, strengthening the souls of the disciples, encouraging them to continue in the faith, and saying that *through many tribulations we must enter the kingdom of God.* (Acts 14:21–22)

Paul did not try to soften the claims that Jesus put on his followers. He did not use a bait-and-switch tactic by luring people with the promise of prosperity and then changing his tune when trouble arrived. He said plainly, "All who desire to live a godly life in Christ Jesus will be persecuted" (2 Tim. 3:12).

When tribulation began, he reminded the believers that they were not entering something unusual. They were not being singled out because of some sin. They were experiencing what God had ordained for his beloved children. So he urged them not to be "moved by these afflictions. For you yourselves know that we are destined for this" (1 Thess. 3:3).

Seeing Personal Suffering through the Lens of God's Purposes

Paul helped people see their suffering through the lens of God's good purposes for their eternal good:

> We ourselves boast about you in the churches of God for your steadfastness and faith in all your persecutions and in the afflictions that you are enduring. This is evidence of the righteous judgment of God, *that you may be considered worthy of the kingdom of God, for which you are also suffering.* (2 Thess. 1:4–5)

Paul helped individual Christians not just in the pain of persecution but in all their sufferings, whether disease or accident or loss or the ordinary burdens of life. He explained that the whole creation is groaning under futility caused by the fall (Rom. 8:22) and then added that Christians are not exempt from this groaning:

> We know that the whole creation has been groaning together in the pains of childbirth until now. And not only the creation, but we ourselves, who have the firstfruits of the Spirit, groan inwardly as we wait eagerly for adoption as sons, the redemption of our bodies. (Rom. 8:22–23)

In other words, Christians endure groans of almost every kind in this world until Christ comes to redeem our bodies. Life in the body—life in this fallen world—means groaning. So take heart, if you are trusting in Christ. Your suffering is not owing to God's wrath against you. Your condemnation for sin has been taken away by the death of Christ (Rom. 8:1). God will not let you be tested beyond what he gives you the grace to bear (1 Cor. 10:13; 2 Cor. 9:8). Your groaning is limited. Redemption is coming. "Weeping may tarry for the night, but joy comes with the morning" (Ps. 30:5).

Why Is the Whole Creation Groaning?

Amazingly, Paul is eager not only to help us individually, with our personal suffering in the moment, but also with the big picture of why the whole creation is in such a mess. Here is the key passage from his great letter to the Romans:

> The creation was subjected to futility, not willingly, but because of him who subjected it, in hope that the creation itself will be set free from its bondage to corruption and obtain the freedom of the glory of the children of God. For we

know that the whole creation has been groaning together
in the pains of childbirth until now. (Rom. 8:20–22)

This subjection of the creation to futility is a reference to
God's act in the garden of Eden, after Adam and Eve turned
away from God's goodness and wisdom and authority. God did
what he said he would do (Gen. 2:17): he introduced death into
the world and put creation under *bondage to corruption* and
pervasive *futility*. In other words, God's judgment upon the sin
of human rebellion was the breakdown of nature's beautiful
functioning. Now things go wrong. Corruption and futility are
shot through the created order with every manner of suffering
and dying.

The World's Physical Suffering for Human Moral Evil?

We can shed some light on God's purpose in this subjection of
creation if we ask, Why would God's judgment fall on *physical* creation when the sin was an act of the *human heart*? My
answer is that physical miseries of the creation are a visible and
deeply felt witness to the moral ugliness and outrage of sin.

For most of us, the sins of our hearts (our preference for
God's gifts over God himself) do not cause great agony of soul.
We do not feel the real outrage of the universe—namely, that
the beautiful Creator and sustainer of the world is disregarded
and dishonored. But just let our bodies be touched by pain, and
we are full of indignation that this is happening.

In other words, God subjected the physical world to corruption to show us the outrage of sin at the one point where
we really feel it. All physical pain and sorrow should scream
at us, "This is how horrible sin is." This is how serious our
moral condition is before God. This is why the redemption of
the world was not cheap, but cost the infinite price of the Son
of God dying for sinners.

Global Vision and Personal Empathy

It is beautiful and rare when a person can offer a global explanation for suffering, and then also make his own very personal suffering a means of our comfort. But Paul has done this for me many times. He wanted it this way:

> If we are afflicted, it is for your comfort and salvation; and if we are comforted, it is for your comfort, which you experience when you patiently endure the same sufferings that we suffer. (2 Cor. 1:6)

I take this very personally. I love him for the vastness of his global vision. And I love him for turning his own suffering into a means of my comfort.

18

The Horror of Human Sin, the Hope of Human Splendor

Paul had a profound understanding of human nature, not only in its original and libertine and legalistic forms of sinfulness, but also in its capacities for redeemed beauty and glorious destiny.

I suppose we would all agree that there are many folks—including Christians—whose view of human nature is uniformly grim and pessimistic; and there are others whose view is so uniformly optimistic that they think all human problems arise from human circumstances, not human nature. There are Scrooges, and there are Pollyannas.

The Bleakness and the Beauty of Human Nature

Paul does not fall into either of these categories. He held a more negative view of depraved human nature than most people can fathom, and a more exalted view of human destiny than most people can dream.

This utter realism about human sinfulness, combined with a spectacular vision of human splendor, draws me into Paul's sway. He is not easily categorized. Just when you read some pessimistic word about human evil, you see some beautiful portrait of where it is all heading.

Bleak

Paul did not play favorites. He included the religious, the moral, and the poor in the same assessment of spiritual deadness as the most irreligious and immoral and rich. Notice the last five words of this universal indictment of human nature:

> You were dead in the trespasses and sins in which you once walked . . . sons of disobedience—among whom we all once lived . . . by nature children of wrath, *like the rest of mankind.* (Eph. 2:1–3)

The root of our problem is not ignorance. Beneath ignorance is hardness of heart against God and his ways. When I bore down to the bottom of my own sinfulness, with Paul's help, I see at the root not innocent *ignorance* of the good I should do, but hardness against the good I *know.*

> They are darkened in their understanding, alienated from the life of God because of the ignorance that is in them, *due to their hardness of heart.* (Eph. 4:18)

This hardness may take the form of throwing God's law away and becoming debauched in glaring lawlessness (Rom. 1:28–32), or in using God's law to bolster my religious and moral pride (Rom. 2:1–5). No one escapes this disease of sin. We are all infected, because the infection has come down to the human race from our first parents, who sinned against God. This is what we call *original sin.* Paul saw it and taught it.

Beautiful

But, astonishingly, he taught that this world's fallenness is part of a plan to reverse the world's misery. Through Adam, all humanity became sinful, and all creation fell under the curse of death and a thousand sorrows. But at the very point where Paul introduces Adam this way, he portrays Christ as the second Adam. In Christ a new humanity—all who receive his grace—would be rescued from condemnation and inherit eternal life.

> For if, because of one man's trespass, death reigned through that one man, much more will those who receive the abundance of grace and the free gift of righteousness reign in life through the one man Jesus Christ. (Rom. 5:17)

In other words, depravity and misery will not have the last word in this world—indeed, in the whole cosmos. God did not create humanity in vain. In Jesus Christ our destiny is beyond imagination. "What no eye has seen, nor ear heard, nor the heart of man imagined . . . God has prepared for those who love him" (1 Cor. 2:9). Literally *unimaginable.*

The whole creation will be renewed. No more natural disasters. No more environmental degradation. No more pandemics. And all of this renewal of creation is precisely for the sake of the habitation and enjoyment of the sons of God, whose sins are forgiven in Christ and who are brought to moral perfection by the Spirit of God.

> For the creation waits with eager longing for the revealing of *the sons of God.* For the creation was subjected to futility, not willingly, but because of him who subjected it, in hope that the creation itself will be set free from its bondage to corruption and obtain the freedom of the glory of *the children of God.* (Rom. 8:19–21)

Until that day, those who "receive the abundance of grace and the free gift of righteousness" through faith in Christ (Rom. 5:17) will not strut with pride but will be humbled that their inheritance is utterly free and undeserved, bought by the blood of Jesus. This is a spectacular, but humbling, hope:

> Let no one boast in men. For all things are yours, whether Paul or Apollos or Cephas or the world or life or death or the present or the future—all are yours, and you are Christ's, and Christ is God's. (1 Cor. 3:21–23)

The Ring of Truth

When I consider the sweep of Paul's vision of humanity, with its deeply sinful nature and its spectacular future, something clicks. This has the ring of truth. This fits with what I see in history, what I see in the news, and what I see in my own heart. It's not just the sober assessment of our fallenness. And it's not just the vision of a glorious future. It's the combination, and the person of Jesus Christ as the fulcrum where everything tilts from despairing depravity to glorious hope. I find this vision, and the man who saw it and lived it and suffered for it, totally compelling.

19

Showing the Truth of Christian Freedom, but Not in a Simplistic Way

Paul did not oversimplify the complexities of Christian freedom and submission. The call he gave to all Christians—to be subject to proper human authorities—he practiced himself. Yet he lived and preached the truth that only in Christ is there true freedom—"free from all and servant to all."

The word *simplistic* exists because there are kinds of guidance and kinds of explanations that are too simple to account for the real complexities of life. They are *simplistic*. We admire people who can make complex realities simple. But we don't admire *simplistic* counselors or preachers or teachers. They just don't seem to be living in the real world, where things are often very messy. In all my reading of Paul over the years, he has never struck me as simplistic. A good example is the way he deals with our submission to authority in this world alongside our Christian freedom.

Citizenship in Heaven, Therefore . . . ?

It is a fundamental Christian reality that God "has delivered us from the domain of darkness and transferred us to the kingdom of his beloved Son" (Col. 1:13). Because Christians are united to Christ, there is a real sense in which we have already died with him and been raised with him and are already secure in heaven with him.

> If then you have been raised with Christ, seek the things that are above, where Christ is, seated at the right hand of God. Set your minds on things that are above, not on things that are on earth. For you have died, and your life is hidden with Christ in God. (Col. 3:1–3)

Paul draws out this radical implication from Christians' union with Christ:

> Our citizenship is in heaven, and from it we await a Savior, the Lord Jesus Christ, who will transform our lowly body to be like his glorious body, by the power that enables him even to subject all things to himself. (Phil. 3:20–21)

A simplistic inference from this reality would be that Christians have no responsibilities to this world or its institutions. That is not Paul's view. Instead, it seems that, in this freedom from the world, we are sent by God back into the world to be subject to its institutions "for the Lord's sake" (1 Pet. 2:13)—or, as Paul says, "out of reverence for Christ" (Eph. 5:21).

Submission in the State, the Job, the Home

Though your citizenship is in heaven, you nevertheless assume the role of a responsible citizen in your own country: "Let every person be subject to the governing authorities. For there is no authority except from God, and those that exist have been instituted by God" (Rom. 13:1). See the hand of your heavenly Father behind the hand of human government, and submit for his sake.

Similarly, in the socioeconomic sphere, submit to human authorities and turn your service of them into the service of Christ:

> Bondservants, obey your earthly masters with fear and trembling, with a sincere heart, *as you would Christ*, not by the way of eye-service, as people-pleasers, but *as bondservants of Christ*, doing the will of God from the heart, rendering service with a good will *as to the Lord* and not to man. (Eph. 6:5–7)

Is it not amazing how interwoven allegiance to Christ is with allegiance to earthly authorities? This is not simplistic. It is complex, and it will sooner or later result in tensions, even to the breaking point.

Similarly in the home: "Wives, submit to your own husbands, *as to the Lord*" (Eph. 5:22). "Children, obey your parents *in the Lord*" (Eph. 6:1).

Always Free and Always Serving

To be sure, since Christ has come and died and risen to reign over the world, our absolute allegiance to him relativizes all other allegiances. That is, we serve in all other relationships at *his* bidding ultimately, not theirs. Which means that wherever those relationships contradict what he calls us to do, his authority takes precedence.

In a real sense, we are free from these institutions, even while submitting to them. Here's how Paul expressed this:

> Were you a bondservant when called? Do not be concerned about it. (But if you can gain your freedom, avail yourself of the opportunity.) For he who was called in the Lord as a bondservant *is a freedman of the Lord*. Likewise he who was free when called is *a bondservant of Christ*. You were bought with a price; *do not become bondservants of men*. (1 Cor. 7:21–23)

And again: "You are not your own, for you were bought with a price. So glorify God in your body" (1 Cor. 6:19–20). Christ purchased us by his own blood (Acts 20:28). Therefore, he owns us. Therefore, all other claims on our lives are secondary. We stay in them at Christ's bidding and for his sake, not because they have any intrinsic right over us.

For Freedom Christ Has Set You Free

This Christian freedom goes right to the heart of who we are as Christ's people. It goes deeper than freedom from institutions. It is also freedom from the law of God as a way of getting right with God. When Christ died for us, he paid the penalty that the law of God demands for our guilt (Rom. 5:8–9; 8:3). And he fulfilled all the obedience that the law demands for our righteousness (Rom. 5:19). Therefore, we are free! And we dare not return to law-keeping as a way of getting right with God. When we do what God commands, we do so because we are already right with God through faith in Christ, not to get right. So Paul says:

> For freedom Christ has set us free; stand firm therefore, and do not submit again to a yoke of slavery. Look: I, Paul, say to you that if you accept circumcision [law-keeping],

Christ will be of no advantage to you. I testify again to every man who accepts circumcision that he is obligated to keep the whole law. (Gal. 5:1–3)

He Knows the Way of Love

So we are free from God's law and free from the world's institutions—even those ordained by God (e.g., state, business, home). Christ owns us and we are his. He is our absolute commander and protector. If he calls us to submit to any law or any institution, we do it. Not because the institution is absolute. And not because law-keeping makes us right with God. We do it because we believe Christ knows the way of love better than we do. This is what's behind Paul's amazing word, "Though I am free from all, I have made myself a servant to all, that I might win more of them" (1 Cor. 9:19).

Perhaps this gives you a taste for what I mean when I say that Paul is not simplistic. Christians are free—gloriously free in Christ. But to the world our lives may look very much like the lives of mere servants, constantly subordinating our own comforts to the needs of others. "Let each of you look not only to his own interests, but also to the interests of others" (Phil. 2:4). But in God's eyes, this life of love and service is the freest of all. It is not a simplistic reality. But it is beautiful, flowing directly from the cross of Christ. I love Paul for helping me taste this complex beauty.

PART 5

A PERSONAL PASSION
FOR PRECIOUS
COMMUNITY

20

Not Lonely at the Top, but Linked with Precious Friends

Paul's personal connectedness was remarkable, especially in view of how seldom he saw some of his friends, and how exalted his thoughts and his position in the church were.

You have heard it said, "It's lonely at the top." It means that CEOs, and senior pastors, and leaders of non-profit organizations, and politicians in positions of great authority, and scholars at the top of their field, and athletes and actors and musicians who are known by millions—all these live in a rarified atmosphere of isolation from real, relaxed, vulnerable, reciprocal relationships.

This may be owing partly to the way employees or fans put the leader on an unapproachable pedestal; and it may be owing partly to the leaders themselves acting like they are on such a pedestal as part of their persona and power. It may be owing to people's experience of awe and perceptions of aloofness, and it may be owing to the leaders' self-imposed schedule that leaves no room for relationships to grow. It may be owing to felt intimidation (real or unreal), and it may be owing to a leader's personality that is at home with pressure and tasks and ill at ease in ordinary personal dealings that have no authority structures or productivity goals.

Unpretentious Power

But then there is the rare leader who looks you in the eye, and remembers your name, and asks you questions about your life, and gets down to talk to your children, and doesn't worry about the stain on his shirt from lunch. You marvel that he carries his power so unpretentiously. You like him.

Everyone knew that Paul wielded extraordinary authority in the Christian churches. He was at the top. Other apostles held equal authority, but none held more. None had greater gifts. You can feel the power he wields when he says in 1 Corinthians 14:37–38:

> If anyone thinks that he is a prophet, or spiritual, he should acknowledge that the things I am writing to you are a command of the Lord. If anyone does not recognize this, he is not recognized.

That statement would be arrogant if the Lord of the universe, Jesus Christ, hadn't called and commissioned Paul as his ambassador (Acts 26:16–18). It would still be arrogant if Paul used this power to lord it over the churches. Instead, he was deeply aware, as he says in 2 Corinthians 10:8, that his was an "authority, which the Lord gave for building you up and not for destroying you."

From this deep conviction, he said, "Not that we lord it over your faith, but we work with you for your joy" (2 Cor. 1:24).

He did not crave for people to take note of his power. In fact, he said, "This is how one should regard us, as servants [literally *slaves*] of Christ and stewards of the mysteries of God" (1 Cor. 4:1).

A Friendly Giant

Nevertheless, Paul moved among the churches as a giant, which makes his relational connectedness all the more remarkable. Consider one instance—namely, the closing chapter of his greatest letter, Romans. Scan your eyes over his personal greetings:

> Greet my beloved Epaenetus, who was the first convert to Christ in Asia. Greet Mary, who has worked hard for you. Greet Andronicus and Junia, my kinsmen and my fellow prisoners. They are well known to the apostles, and they were in Christ before me. Greet Ampliatus, my beloved in the Lord. Greet Urbanus, our fellow worker in Christ, and my beloved Stachys. Greet Apelles, who is approved in Christ. Greet those who belong to the family of Aristobulus. Greet my kinsman Herodion. Greet those in the Lord who belong to the family of Narcissus. Greet those workers in the Lord, Tryphaena and Tryphosa. Greet the beloved Persis, who has worked hard in the Lord. Greet Rufus, chosen in the Lord; also his mother, who has been a mother to me as well. Greet Asyncritus, Phlegon, Hermes, Patrobas, Hermas, and the brothers who are with them. Greet Philologus, Julia, Nereus and his sister, and Olympas, and all the saints who are with them. Greet one another with a holy kiss. All the churches of Christ greet you. (Rom. 16:5–16)

Sixteen times in twelve verses he says, "Greet." Whenever we talk like this, at least three people are involved. In this case, there is Paul, and there are those he is writing to, and there is the person or group he wants them to greet. What's happening in this three-part connection? Something is being carried by the middle person from Paul to the third person. What is being carried? Yes, a greeting. But what's the point of a greeting? The point of the greeting is *love*.

Four times he says it explicitly: "my beloved" (vv. 5, 8, 9, 12). Paul loves these people. That's what this text is about. Paul is saying, "I love these people, and I want my love to be carried from my heart to their heart by you. So please take these words from me and make them the bottle from which you pour my love into their lives—twenty-six different friends."

What Leader Is Like This?

Amazing. I've *never* written a letter like this. I've never asked a friend to greet twenty-six people by name. Nor have I *read* anything like this in any biography or memoir. This personal connectedness is rare. From the most influential Christian leader in the first century—a man at the top—we see a relational connectedness that fills us with wonder. He had never even been to Rome, where all these people were living! He had met them elsewhere, but followed their travels and knew their situation.

Here is a man who did not let his authority, or his being at the top, choke off the affections that he felt for these friends. You cannot help but feel, as you read this final chapter of Romans (with all its exalted thoughts about God), that these friends were precious to Paul. This was not politics. This was personal affection and love. The kind of love that two thousand years later draws out the same in us—for him.

21

Christ Was All-Sufficient, and Community Was Crucial

In spite of all the authority and esteem Paul had in the early church, and in spite of all the expectations that he would meet the spiritual needs of others, Paul practiced what he preached when he said that no Christian can say to others, "I have no need of you." He yearned for the encouragement and strengthening he received from others.

Paul refers to himself as an apostle of Jesus sixteen times in his thirteen letters in the New Testament. This was the highest title of authority in the early church under Jesus himself (1 Cor. 14:37–38), but it also implied that Paul would be utterly spent or poured out for the good of the churches. The authority was not for lording it over the churches, but for serving them and building them up, at great cost to the apostles.

Authoritative and Needed
Paul was an authority by office, but a servant by function. And the service was draining:

Even if I am to be poured out as a drink offering upon the sacrificial offering of your faith, I am glad and rejoice with you all. (Phil. 2:17)

I will most gladly spend and be spent for your souls. (2 Cor. 12:15)

I rejoice in my sufferings for your sake, and in my flesh I am filling up what is lacking in Christ's afflictions for the sake of his body, that is, the church. (Col. 1:24)

Being affectionately desirous of you, we were ready to share with you not only the gospel of God but also our own selves, because you had become very dear to us. (1 Thess. 2:8)

I endure everything for the sake of the elect, that they also may obtain the salvation that is in Christ Jesus with eternal glory. (2 Tim. 2:10)

In other words, Christ called his apostles so they could meet others' needs. The focus of an apostle was not on his own need of others, but on their need of him. His authority was for building others up (2 Cor. 10:8; 13:10), not for the sake of getting others to serve him. An apostle depended on Jesus—both for his authority and for his strength. "I can do all things through him who strengthens me" (Phil. 4:13).

Individualism or Interdependence?

There seems to be something admirable in a Christ-dependent person who can continually give and give and give to others without receiving anything back. In one sense, this makes Christ look great. He is all-sufficient to supply what his servant needs.

But that's not the way Christ set up his church. He did not will that every follower be a rugged, independent individual who needs no other mere human but gets all his resources directly from Christ. That may sound Christ-exalting. But it isn't. Here's what Paul taught the Corinthians about mutual interdependence in the body of Christ:

> God arranged the members in the body, each one of them, as he chose. If all were a single member, where would the body be? As it is, there are many parts, yet one body. The eye cannot say to the hand, "I have no need of you," nor again the head to the feet, "I have no need of you." On the contrary, the parts of the body that seem to be weaker are indispensable. (1 Cor. 12:18–22)

Paul Was Included in the Interdependent

So no Christian can say to another Christian, "I have no need of you." That includes Paul. Apostles are as much a part of the body as anyone. Christ has chosen to glorify himself by being the head of the body. That is, he will be the decisive, ultimate leader and supplier of all things—not directly, but through the members of his body to the other members of the body:

> We are to grow up in every way into him who is the head, into Christ, from whom the whole body, joined and held together by every joint with which it is equipped, when each part is working properly, makes the body grow so that it builds itself up in love. (Eph. 4:15–16)

How easy it would be to imagine a man of great authority and power and esteem thinking that he himself is above the ordinary means of grace that he says others need. But not Paul. He is unashamed to express his need for other Christians:

> I long to see you, that I may impart to you some spiritual gift to strengthen you—that is, that we may be mutually

encouraged by each other's faith, both yours and mine. (Rom. 1:11–12)

I hope to see you in passing as I go to Spain, and to be helped on my journey there by you, once I have enjoyed your company for a while. (Rom. 15:24)

Since we were torn away from you, brothers, for a short time, in person not in heart, we endeavored the more eagerly and with great desire to see you face to face. . . . For what is our hope or joy or crown of boasting before our Lord Jesus at his coming? Is it not you? For you are our glory and joy. (1 Thess. 2:17–20)

If I cause you pain, who is there to make me glad but the one whom I have pained? (2 Cor. 2:2)

As I remember your tears, I long to see you, that I may be filled with joy. (2 Tim. 1:4)

One measure of the greatness of a man is not only that he practices what he preaches, but also that he doesn't consider himself above the ordinary means of grace that all Christians need, including the fellowship of other believers. Paul bears his authority and power and reputation without pretense, and freely admits his need for the refreshment of Christ that comes through other believers. His commands are the more compelling for his own compliance with them. His humble need for, and delight in, the friendship and partnership of others makes him all the more winsome.

22

Backbone, Blunt, and Beautifully Affirming

Paul could manifest the most tender affection in dealing with his churches, without losing the ability to be utterly blunt and forceful when necessary.

Most of us know people who are blunt. Sometimes their bluntness morphs into harshness and unkindness. If that happens often enough, we may sense that they have a kind of personality disorder, because they seem unable to express emotions other than frustration and anger. They give little positive affirmation and little praise—of anything. There is little spontaneous expression of the sort of joy that is self-forgetful and simply swept up into some wonderful experience.

On the other hand, most of us know people who are always chipper, always smiling, always commending, always gentle and kind. We marvel at this. It seems wonderful and biblical. But then, over time, we may sense that something is amiss.

These people never seem to notice the wrongs others do. They seem to never take note of evils and injustices in society. They are silent when others are wrestling with a difficult moral issue. They don't give their opinion when there is a matter of church discipline, where a church member is guilty of unrepentant wrong. They seem incapable of disagreeing or correcting or admonishing. They are only positive or silent.

What we once saw as a beautiful trait of kindness starts to seem like a lopsided mark of insecurity. A lack of conviction or moral backbone. A fear of conflict. A desperate need to have everything smooth and positive. A need to be seen positively, and a quiet dread of being criticized or rejected. And gradually we realize that there is something unhealthy behind this smiling face.

Lavish in Affirmation, Direct in Criticism

What we want to see in others, and have in ourselves, is a kind of wholeness that can be blunt and forceful and corrective when necessary, but that also has a peaceful pattern of encouragement and affirmation and kindness. Expressions of anger are common and unexceptional in our world. Most people are capable of expressing anger. But what we want is a predominant kindness that is just as capable of expressing positive emotions like thankfulness, and admiration, and hopeful expectancy, and exultation over good news, and heartfelt empathy, and sorrow over bad news.

Paul was one of those people who was lavish in his commendations and direct in his criticisms. For example, the church at Corinth was a troubled church, with conflicts over leaders, church discipline, food offered to pagan idols, the Lord's Supper, the role of women in worship, the use of spiritual gifts, and more. In short, the church gave Paul headaches of concern

(2 Cor. 11:28). But listen to his opening paragraph in his first letter to them.

> I give thanks to my God always for you because of the grace of God that was given you in Christ Jesus, that in every way you were enriched in him in all speech and all knowledge—even as the testimony about Christ was confirmed among you—so that you are not lacking in any gift, as you wait for the revealing of our Lord Jesus Christ, who will sustain you to the end, guiltless in the day of our Lord Jesus Christ. God is faithful, by whom you were called into the fellowship of his Son, Jesus Christ our Lord. (1 Cor. 1:4–9)

Paul expressed this kind of robust affirmation not only in his letters. We all know that some people can *write* kind words, but *in person* they are emotionally ham-fisted. Paul could be as emotionally warm and expressive in person as he was in his letters. For example, he writes to the Thessalonian church:

> We were gentle among you, like a nursing mother taking care of her own children. So, being affectionately desirous of you, we were ready to share with you not only the gospel of God but also our own selves, because you had become very dear to us. (1 Thess. 2:7–8)

But when the time was right, Paul could be utterly blunt and forceful in his reprimands. For example, after that warm commendatory beginning, Paul later says to the Corinthians, "In the following instructions I do not commend you" (1 Cor. 11:17). That is clear and straightforward and blunt.

Blunt, Brief, Forgiving

Paul was keenly aware of the limits of rebuke and correction. Such treatment should be brief and redemptive if at all possible.

Listen to his concern about a disciplined brother, whose discipline he himself had encouraged:

> This punishment by the majority is enough, so you should rather turn to forgive and comfort him, or he may be overwhelmed by excessive sorrow. So I beg you to reaffirm your love for him. (2 Cor. 2:6–8)

Beautiful. But all the more beautiful because Paul had the moral backbone and the emotional ability to say, "I do not commend you," and, "I thank God for you. He will sustain you to the end." This kind of robust emotional well-roundedness draws out my heart in admiration and love to this extraordinary man.

23

Zeal for Gospel Accuracy, Slow to Take Personal Offense

In spite of Paul's intense commitment to gospel accuracy, he was astonishingly tolerant of those who preached the true gospel with defective motives, even those who wanted to hurt him.

I don't fully understand everything about Paul. I admit to feeling mainly admiration for him on this point, but I have also been perplexed. Let me try to help you see why.

Angry and Baffled

Galatians is Paul's most severe letter. He is, it appears, quite angry—not at the believers in Galatia, but at those who have come from Jerusalem and are teaching a different gospel that sounds Christ-honoring, but which Paul knows cannot save the sinful soul. To the believers he is more baffled than angry:

O foolish Galatians! Who has bewitched you? It was before your eyes that Jesus Christ was publicly portrayed as crucified. . . . Did you suffer so many things in vain—if indeed it was in vain? . . . How can you turn back again to the weak and worthless elementary principles of the world, whose slaves you want to be once more? You observe days and months and seasons and years! I am afraid I may have labored over you in vain. (Gal. 3:1, 4; 4:9–11)

But to the false teachers who are misleading the believers, Paul is not baffled. He is angry. He would no doubt say, "If a wolf is scattering the sheep, you get angry at the wolf, not the sheep." Here is one of the most severe parts of the letter:

I am astonished that you are so quickly deserting him who called you in the grace of Christ and are turning to a different gospel—not that there is another one, but there are some who trouble you and want to distort the gospel of Christ. But even if we or an angel from heaven should preach to you a gospel contrary to the one we preached to you, let him be accursed. As we have said before, so now I say again: If anyone is preaching to you a gospel contrary to the one you received, let him be accursed. (Gal. 1:6–9)

Paul does not often call down a curse on false teachers. This passage is the most severe. Without the gospel people will perish. These people are undermining the gospel. Therefore, they are destroying people. Paul says that is what should happen to them—destruction—if they go on perverting the gospel of Christ.

Rejoicing Over the Preaching of Unloving Preachers

Now, keep all that in mind and look with me at another situation where Paul's adversaries are preaching to Christians.

His response is strikingly different. Why? He is in prison in Rome when he writes the letter to the Philippians. He wants to encourage them that God turns even imprisonment for the advance of the gospel. So he points out, "Most of the brothers, having become confident in the Lord by my imprisonment, are much more bold to speak the word without fear" (Phil. 1:14). So far, so good. That is indeed encouraging. Then he adds this:

> Some indeed preach Christ from envy and rivalry, but others from good will. The latter do it out of love, knowing that I am put here for the defense of the gospel. The former proclaim Christ out of selfish ambition, not sincerely but thinking to afflict me in my imprisonment. What then? Only that in every way, whether in pretense or in truth, Christ is proclaimed, and in that I rejoice. (Phil. 1:15–18)

So in Galatia people are preaching a different gospel—one that makes justification stand on law-keeping, not on Christ alone received by faith—and Paul is jealous enough for the safety of the believers that he calls down a curse on the false teachers. But here in Philippians, Paul hears about preachers who do not love him and want to make him more miserable in prison, but instead of cursing them, he says, "I rejoice that Christ is being preached."

The part of this that I find admirable is that Paul's anger in Galatians is not a personal pique, but a love for the sheep amid wolves. We know it's not a personal resentment because the Philippian situation really does present an opportunity for personal resentment, but Paul doesn't take it. He rejoices.

Elevating Accuracy, Not Irritability

So the difference between the two situations really does show Paul to be wonderfully principled rather than easily irritated at personal offenses. The Galatian false teachers were ruining people by perverting the gospel itself. The Philippian rascals were preaching the very gospel Paul preached (at least, he raised no objections), but they were doing it precisely because he couldn't, and they wanted him to be irritated. This Paul could handle. It was the purity of the gospel that mattered, not whether his feelings got hurt.

When I see this kind of principled response in Galatians and Philippians, I love what I see. I want to be that jealous for gospel accuracy and that free from personal self-regard.

But Doesn't Unloving Preaching Matter?

What baffles me is that Paul seems to just let the sinfulness of the preachers in Rome go. It's true that they were not distorting the gospel in their preaching, but they were distorting it in their attitudes. What are we to make of this? Aren't actions and attitudes also important in presenting the gospel, not just correct words? In Galatians, Peter's conduct "was not in step with the truth of the gospel" (Gal. 2:14), and in Rome, the unloving preachers' attitudes were not in step with the truth of the gospel.

I have two suggestions in answer to this question. One is that Paul really does think that if the message of the gospel itself goes wrong, all talk of the preacher being a good person becomes moot. Paul says that even an angel from heaven, with all his moral perfection, could not save a single soul with a corrupted gospel (Gal. 1:8).

On the other hand, an unkind, resentful, immature preacher who preaches an accurate and true gospel of the grace of God may be the instrument of salvation. We can't miss the implication. Paul really does think that salvation is more thoroughly undermined by a corrupted gospel than by a corrupted preacher.

Circling Back with Devastating Clarity about Their Sin

But the second suggestion I have is that Paul was not indifferent to the attitudes of the adversaries in the letter to the Philippians. Virtually every sentence in the letter is a rebuke to their selfishness. For example:

> Do nothing from selfish ambition or conceit, but in humility count others more significant than yourselves. Let each of you look not only to his own interests, but also to the interests of others. (Phil. 2:3–4)

This is the whole drift of the letter, which means that Paul made a tactical decision in Philippians 1 when mentioning the adversaries who want to afflict him in his imprisonment. Instead of stopping to chasten them, which was not at all the point at the moment, he takes the moral high ground of patience and grace, and then later circles back to show how wrong the attitudes of the adversaries were. In this way he hopes, perhaps, to win them back by admonishing them indirectly rather than directly.

Demanding Writing, Pastoral Wisdom

So the more I have thought about Paul's handling of the Galatian situation (behind the letter to the Galatians) and the Roman situation (behind the letter to the Philippians), the more they merge into admiration. He was indeed jealous for gospel accuracy, and he was indeed concerned for gospel love and humility and kindness. His peculiar way of responding to both is a mark not of inconsistency but of pastoral wisdom.

I must admit that my love for Paul comes partly from the fact that almost every time he baffles me, further reflection brings resolution and deeper insight. He is a very demanding thinker and writer. I admire this, even though I am often baffled—at least at first. Now add to this the pastoral wisdom that guides his demanding mind for gracious purposes. All this is on display in Philippians. The upshot for me is a mingling of admiration and affection. In other words, I love him for it.

24

Not a Conforming Chameleon, and Not a Ministering Maverick

Though Paul was driven by an extraordinary ambition— "to preach the gospel, not where Christ has already been named"— he was not a lone-wolf kind of leader. He believed in teams and never intended to travel alone or do his mission work without living in some kind of supportive Christian community.

We in the modern West—I mean the last three hundred years or so—have a love affair with the strong, independent, self-sufficient, self-assertive hero who accomplishes great feats against all odds, with little help from others. Some biblical virtues are entangled in the fabric of that heroic life. But as a whole, it is not the kind of life that Paul extolled or encouraged or modeled.

"Two by Two"—the Principle of Teams

Even when thinking biblically, none of us admires a chameleon, who has no independent identity but instead follows the path of expediency by fitting in to the expectations of whatever company he's in, no matter how questionable. Or, to change the animal image, none of us is attracted to a person who is more like a jellyfish than a dolphin. Floating with the current of the times, with no backbone to swim against the tide of evil, is not admirable.

Paul was not a chameleon. Chameleons don't get stoned and whipped and imprisoned and martyred. They conform. On the other hand, Paul was not a maverick. He was not the kind of free spirit who said, "A pox on your house! I'm going to Spain, like it or not."

When you study Paul's missionary travels, it seems that Paul took to heart the practice of Jesus to send his disciples on their journeys in pairs. Jesus endorsed and Paul embraced the principle of missionary teams. Jesus had sent out his twelve apostles "two by two" (Mark 6:7). Even when he sent larger numbers of workers, he did the same: "The Lord appointed seventy-two others and sent them on ahead of him, two by two, into every town and place where he himself was about to go" (Luke 10:1). In doing this, Jesus did not encourage the vision of fearless, independent mavericks conquering the world one by one.

Never Alone in Ministry by Choice

In Paul's entire ministry, as we read about it in his letters and in the book of Acts, he always traveled and ministered with others. The instances that look like they might be exceptions only prove the rule when you examine them closely.

For example, Paul and Silas and Timothy were ministering together in Thessalonica. When it looked like the people were going to riot, Paul and Silas left for the nearby town of Berea. But the troublemakers followed them there. The danger became so severe that Paul was sent *alone* to Athens by sea (Acts 17:13–14).

But Luke, the author of Acts, is careful to record Paul's reaction to this departure: "Those who conducted Paul brought him as far as Athens, and *after receiving a command for Silas and Timothy to come to him as soon as possible*, they departed" (Acts 17:15). In other words, under pressure, Paul was willing to be sent away alone to protect his life, but this was not the way he intended to do ministry, and he ordered the quick arrival of his ministry partners.

Another example is when Paul and his longtime associate Barnabas could not agree on whether to take on their journey John Mark, who had left them on a previous journey. Paul said no. Barnabas said yes. Luke, painfully and honestly, reports the dispute:

> There arose a sharp disagreement, so that they separated from each other. Barnabas took Mark with him and sailed away to Cyprus, but Paul chose Silas and departed, having been commended by the brothers to the grace of the Lord. (Acts 15:39–40)

In other words, even though the dispute broke up one missionary team, neither Barnabas nor Paul had any intention of striking out on his own without a partner. They were both committed to ministry in teams.

Even Powerful Dolphins Swim in Pods

As I examine my own heart and the bent I have to admire rugged individualists, I realize that these lone heroes display a kind of courage and conviction that I ought to admire. You can't be a mature, fruitful Christian without these traits. But then I realize that I admire such courage and conviction and dolphin-like independence from the culture even more when it swims in sweet fellowship with other believers. The ruggedness required to take a stand against sinful culture is the more beautiful when it is tender enough to receive encouragement from a fellow believer. Paul was as rugged and courageous and strong as any man I have ever known. But watch him receive encouragement from one of his partners, Titus:

> Even when we came into Macedonia, our bodies had no rest, but we were afflicted at every turn—fighting without and fear within. But God, who comforts the downcast, comforted us by the coming of Titus. (2 Cor. 7:5–6)

When I see the great apostle, who was undaunted by every danger, happily celebrating the comfort he received from a comrade in the great cause, my admiration of his strength is not diminished but increased. God made us to be interdependent. Jesus structured his missions that way—two by two. And Paul lived it out. I see him as the greater for it. Not weaker.

PART 6

COUNTING OTHERS MORE SIGNIFICANT THAN HIMSELF

25

Lover of God's Sovereignty
with Tears for the Lost

Paul had an incomparably high view of God's sovereignty
in salvation mingled with heartfelt tears for those who
were not saved.

Many religious people in the world believe God is absolutely
sovereign over all things—that he controls the course of history
and governs the lives of individuals. Most Muslims believe this,
and many Christians.

And many Christians believe that people without faith in
Jesus Christ are without salvation, and they feel compassion
for them.

But it is not so common to find people who hold this conviction about God's sovereignty *and* this compassion for the
lost together, profoundly and authentically, in one human
soul. But Paul did hold them together. Paul embraced and
expressed the sovereignty of God over all historical events

and in people's lives. And he embraced the lost world with compassion and longing.

For Paul, God Is Sovereign over Human Acts

In Romans 9:15–18, Paul lays out the absolute sovereignty of God over all human willing:

> [God said,] "I will have mercy on whom I have mercy, and I will have compassion on whom I have compassion" [quoting Ex. 33:19]. So then it depends not on human will or exertion, but on God, who has mercy. For the Scripture says to Pharaoh, "For this very purpose I have raised you up, that I might show my power in you, and that my name might be proclaimed in all the earth" [quoting Ex. 9:16]. So then he has mercy on whomever he wills, and he hardens whomever he wills.

Paul puts God's sovereignty in a phrase in Ephesians 1:11: God "works all things according to the counsel of his will." And he gives the most sweeping statement of all in Romans 11:36: "From him and through him and to him are all things. To him be glory forever."

Paul knew that all of us are spiritually dead and blind in our sin and that our only hope is that an all-powerful God would create in us new light and life (2 Cor. 4:6; Eph. 2:5). Human agents are crucial in the process of our conversion. But God's sovereign grace is decisive: "I planted, Apollos watered, but God gave the growth" (1 Cor. 3:6).

Paul's Great Sorrow and Unceasing Anguish

For some, this news of God's sovereignty in the work of salvation seems to numb their compassion for the lost. Something is deeply wrong when that happens. And we know it is wrong, because for Paul the opposite happened. His confidence in the sovereign grace of God to save the worst of sinners intensified alongside his passionate concern for perishing sinners:

> I am speaking the truth in Christ—I am not lying; my conscience bears me witness in the Holy Spirit—that I have great sorrow and unceasing anguish in my heart. For I could wish that I myself were accursed and cut off from Christ for the sake of my brothers, my kinsmen according to the flesh. (Rom. 9:1–3)

And not only was there "great sorrow" and "anguish" in Paul's heart, but there were prayers overflowing from his lips. The sovereignty of God, for Paul, did not make the pursuit of sinners pointless—it made it hopeful. Nothing in man can stop this sovereign God from saving the worst of sinners: "Brothers, my heart's desire and prayer to God for them is that they may be saved" (Rom. 10:1). The compassion of his heart overflowed in prayer because he knew the sovereign power of God could overcome every obstacle that sinful man raised up against his own salvation.

"Though He Cause Grief, He Will Have Compassion"

I love the sovereignty of God. I love to join the psalmists when they exult in God's unparalleled power: "Be exalted, O LORD, *in your strength*! We will sing and praise *your power*" (Ps. 21:13). I love to join them in God's house as they say, "I have looked upon you in the sanctuary, beholding *your power* and glory" (Ps. 63:2). And the older I get, the more I love to embrace for my own legacy their words: "Even to old age and gray hairs, O God, do not forsake me, until I proclaim *your might* to another generation, *your power* to all those to come" (Ps. 71:18).

And I love the compassion of God. I would be utterly lost without it. I love the refrain that runs through the whole Bible, that in the midst of judgment God remembers mercy (Hab. 3:2). What keeps the Bible from being the bleakest of books, in its utter realism about the rebellion of the human heart, is the unfathomable patience of God: "Yet he, being compassionate, atoned for their iniquity and did not destroy them; he restrained his anger often" (Ps. 78:38).

Psalm 103 is one of my favorite psalms because there is so much hope in it. And that hope is rooted in God's compassion: "As a father shows *compassion* to his children, so the LORD shows *compassion* to those who fear him" (Ps. 103:13). Over and over we hear the joyful sound: "The LORD will . . . *have compassion* on his servants" (Ps. 135:14). "For a brief moment I deserted you, but with *great compassion* I will gather you" (Isa. 54:7).

But the greatest thrill comes from seeing the sovereignty and the compassion of God interwoven in one glorious fabric of justice and mercy. One of the most beautiful and painful statements of this interweaving comes in Lamentations 3:31–33. God had brought horrific judgment on his own city, Jerusalem. No one doubted that this grievous event had come from the sovereign hand of God. But Jeremiah weaves God's sovereignty and compassion together in these amazing words:

> The Lord will not
> cast off forever,
> but, though *he cause grief*, he will *have compassion*
> according to the abundance of his steadfast love;
> for he does not afflict from his heart
> or grieve the children of men.

He caused the grief. He will have the compassion.

His Heart Held Fast the Mystery

The apostle Paul was steeped in this kind of Old Testament teaching. This was the strong flavor of God that he savored. God is sovereign and "works all things according to the counsel of his will" (Eph. 1:11). And God is merciful and compassionate. And we sinners—we are all guilty and helpless and responsible for our sin. If God were not compassionate, he would not *want* to save us. If God were not sovereign, he would not *be able* to save us. But he is both. And because of Jesus we are saved.

It is not essential in this life that we know how to explain the way God's sovereignty and our responsibility fit together. It is enough to know that they do. Paul cherished God's sovereignty to save, and he wept over those who refused to come. He saw and he lived this mystery. His mind was not so small or brittle that it broke while contemplating complex greatness. And for this I love him.

26

Apostle of the Happy God and the Hard Life of Spreading Joy

Of all the magnificent ways Paul hoped his life would count for his churches, he said twice that his aim was their joy. He had found his deepest and most enduring joy in Christ, and he wanted the same for other people.

We are not accustomed to thinking that people with the greatest intellects, and the most logically rigorous theology, and the most carefully worded letters, might also be known for their overflowing joy. And even less would we expect that joy would be the very marrow of their philosophy and capstone of their affections.

Paul, Apostle of the Infinitely Happy God

But Paul shatters our customary expectations. He is a great intellect. His theology is logically rigorous. His wording is careful. And not only is his own joy overflowing, but it is part of the very marrow of his understanding of God's life and ours.

Jesus had portrayed God as the father of a prodigal who threw a party when his son came home (Luke 15:22–24), and he had portrayed himself in the day of judgment as a master who welcomes his servants home with the words "Enter into the joy of your master" (Matt. 25:21).

Now Paul pictures the Christian gospel as "the gospel of the glory of the *happy* God" (1 Tim. 1:11, my translation). And he pronounces a doxology on behalf of this God with the words "he who is the *happy* and only Sovereign, the King of kings and Lord of lords" (1 Tim. 6:15, my translation). The word for *happy* is usually translated *blessed*, but the meaning is not blessed in the sense of "praised," but blessed in the sense of "contented" or "happy."

Trinitarian Joy

Paul knew that a gloomy God could not be the source, let alone the center, of all-satisfying good news. No. If Jesus came into the world with "good news of great joy," as the angels said (Luke 2:10), then God is not a gloomy God, but a God of overflowing joy. This is why the Son whom he sent could say, "These things I have spoken to you, *that my joy may be in you,* and that your joy may be full" (John 15:11; see also 17:13). Joy *originates* in God. It comes *through* Jesus his Son. And it is the *fruit* of his Spirit. Those who embrace Jesus as their Savior and treasure, by the power of the Spirit, for the glory of the Father, enter into that Trinitarian joy. That's what I mean by calling it the "*marrow* of Paul's understanding of God's life and ours."

He Savored Joy before He Spread It—Even in Sorrow

Paul experienced this joy in God before he spread it. He did not experience it intermittently, as if it came only when the sun was shining. Paul's joy was stunningly sturdy in sorrow and suffering. For example, he says, "We *rejoice* in hope of the glory of God. Not only that, but we *rejoice* in our sufferings. . . . More than that, we also *rejoice* in God" (Rom. 5:2–3, 11). He was "sorrowful, yet always *rejoicing*" (2 Cor. 6:10). "In all our affliction, I am overflowing with *joy*" (2 Cor. 7:4). "I will boast all the more *gladly* of my weaknesses, so that the power of Christ may rest upon me" (2 Cor. 12:9).

And beneath all of Paul's exhortations to rejoice, as their foundation, he taught that joy is not a human performance but a "fruit of the Spirit" (Gal. 5:22). It is an effect of God's rule coming into someone's life (Rom. 14:17). It is part of love, the greatest gift of love: "[Love] *rejoices* with the truth" (1 Cor. 13:6).

He Is on the Earth for Their "Joy of Faith"

With these roots, Paul pursued the joy of other people. This was one of the great aims of his preaching—that people would find their supreme joy no longer in this world, but in Christ, just as he had. Twice he stated that the aim of his ministry was the *joy* of his churches. In Philippians 1:23–26, Paul ponders whether he will get his supreme joy by going to be with Jesus in death, or whether he will stay on earth for the joy of the Philippian church. He answers, "I know that I will remain and continue with you all, for your progress and *joy of faith* [my translation], so that in me you may have ample cause to glory in Christ Jesus, because of my coming to you again" (Phil. 1:25–26).

In other words, "If I remain on the earth, the reason will be your *joy of faith*." That is why Paul lives: for the joy of his people in Christ, which is part and parcel of their glorying (or boasting, or exulting) in Christ Jesus. Enjoying Christ and glorying in Christ are not distinct. You can't have one without the other. Bored boasting in Christ and sad exultation in Christ are oxymorons. The enjoyment is essential to making much of Christ. So when Paul lives for the joy of his people in Christ, he is living for the glory of Christ. This is what he meant when he said, in Philippians 1:21, "to live is Christ."

Not over Them, but alongside Them for Their Joy

And again, he said very simply to the Corinthians, "Not that we lord it over your faith, but we work with you *for your joy*" (2 Cor. 1:24). Is this not amazing for an apostle to say? He has supreme authority in the early church, along with the other apostles under Christ. Of all the ways he could describe his goal with the Corinthians, what does he say? He says, negatively, that they don't lord it over them. Then he says two things positively: "We work with you." Not *over*, but *alongside*. Then he says, "We work . . . for your joy." Paul is not ashamed to sum up his ministry goal as "for your joy."

Why would that be? Because joy in Christ—or we could say, *being satisfied with all that God is for us in Jesus*—is the essence of what Christians should pursue in the world. Not the totality of what we pursue, but the *essence*. Christianity is a divine project of replacing inferior joys in inferior objects with superior joys in God himself. That is why Christ came to die. He died to remove every barrier (like God's wrath and our sin) between us and God so that we could say with Paul, "We . . . rejoice in God" (Rom. 5:11).

Faith, Hope, and Love Abide. But Joy?

Someone asked me once, "If joy is so central, why did Paul famously say, 'Now faith, hope, and love abide, these three; but the greatest of these is love' (1 Cor. 13:13), but didn't mention joy?" My answer is that joy is so essential to faith, hope, and love that he didn't need to mention joy. If you take joy, as an essential element, out of faith, hope, or love, you do not have Christian faith, hope, or love. Faith is the *satisfying* embrace of the trusted and treasured Christ. Hope is the *satisfying* foretaste of the future reward. Love is the overflow of *joy* in God that seeks to meet the needs of others, especially the need of eternal joy.

Learning to Love from a Man I Love

My love for Paul rises not only because his joy stood firm through all his sufferings, but even more because he saw his whole ministry as a project of bringing others into the joy that he had in knowing Jesus Christ. This is, in fact, the way Paul understood love—bringing people into his joy in God, no matter what it cost him. So he writes, "I felt sure of all of you, that *my joy would be the joy of you all*. For I wrote to you . . . to let you know *the abundant love that I have for you*" (2 Cor. 2:3–4). Love means gladly embracing the quest to bring others into your experience of joy in God, even if it costs you your life.

Is it a surprise that I would love the man who has shown me more than any other, after Jesus, what love is? And is it a surprise that loving him, and learning to love like him, is such a happy affair?

27

Admitting Imperfections and Turning Them for Love

Paul knew he was not a perfect man, and instead of hiding his flaws, he made them an occasion to help others fight for holiness and joy.

The people we admire most do not put on airs. They do not pretend to be better than they are. If they blunder, they admit it. We do not like pretense or sham or hypocrisy. We like reality. Imperfect people who are honest about their flaws are more likeable, more believable, than even more accomplished people who won't admit their flaws.

Paul was in a very elite group of people—the apostles of Jesus Christ. He did not sign up for this. He said he had been set apart for it by God before he was born: "He . . . set me apart before I was born, and . . . called me by his grace" (Gal. 1:15). To be an apostle meant that he had seen the risen Lord Jesus and had been commissioned by him to speak on his behalf with his authority. This is why his writings have such authority for Christians.

No Christian Perfection in This Life

But in spite of having such a privileged role in the early church, Paul did not try to pull rank by hiding his weaknesses or his sins. He knew and taught that becoming a Christian does not mean sinless perfection in this world. To be sure, becoming a Christian means that people will really be changed by the Spirit of God (2 Cor. 3:18). God is saving his people not only from the *guilt* of sin, but also from its *power*. But this salvation is happening in stages.

First, in this world God brings people out of spiritual darkness (2 Cor. 4:4–6), grants them to repent and believe (2 Tim. 2:25; Phil. 1:29), unites them to Jesus Christ (Rom. 6:5), counts them as having the very righteousness and perfect obedience of Christ (Rom. 5:19), gives them the gift of the Holy Spirit and the gift of eternal life (Rom. 8:9; 6:23), and begins the process of making them like Jesus, from one degree of glory to the next (2 Cor. 3:18). But that process is not completed until Christians get to heaven, or until Jesus comes.

So Paul's aim is to be with Jesus someday, but he admits that he is not there yet and that he is not perfect. "I [aim to] attain the resurrection from the dead. *Not that I have already obtained this or am already perfect*, but I press on to make it my own, because Christ Jesus has made me his own" (Phil. 3:11–12). Paul knew Christ had taken hold of him for eternal life. But he was not yet at the end of his journey. And that journey was one of constant warfare against sin. That's why he writes to his young friend Timothy,

> Fight the good fight of the faith. Take hold of the eternal
> life to which you were called and about which you made

the good confession in the presence of many witnesses. (1 Tim. 6:12)

Paul knew that this whole age is one of incompleteness and imperfection. He puts it like this in one of his most famous chapters:

For we know in part and we prophesy in part, but when the perfect comes, the partial will pass away. . . . For now we see in a mirror dimly, but then face to face. Now I know in part; then I shall know fully, even as I have been fully known. (1 Cor. 13:9–10, 12)

Paul's Most Astonishing Confession

The most astonishing confession Paul ever made of his own imperfections and struggles is in Romans 7:

I do not understand my own actions. For I do not do what I want, but I do the very thing I hate. . . . I know that nothing good dwells in me, that is, in my flesh. . . . I delight in the law of God, in my inner being, but I see in my members another law waging war against the law of my mind. . . . Who will deliver me from this body of death? Thanks be to God through Jesus Christ our Lord! (Rom. 7:15, 18, 22–25)

God had done a stunning work of salvation in Paul. He displayed irrefutable love and self-denial and passion for his Master, Jesus Christ. But God had not yet perfected him.

Why Was Paul Saved So Slowly?

We get a glimpse into why this might be—why God allowed Paul (and the rest of us) to struggle on against temptation. Remember that Paul was chosen by God before he was born to be an apostle (Gal. 1:15). God knew that one day he would break into Paul's life with irresistible force and call him to be his apostle. Nevertheless, God allowed Paul to become a vicious murderer and persecutor of his own Son and his church (Acts 9:1–2).

Why? I am suggesting that the answer to that question is the same answer to why God allowed Paul to go on struggling against sin. Here is Paul's answer:

> Formerly I was a blasphemer, persecutor, and insolent opponent. But I received mercy. . . . The saying is trustworthy and deserving of full acceptance, that Christ Jesus came into the world to save sinners, of whom I am the foremost. But I received mercy for this reason, that in me, as the foremost, Jesus Christ might display his perfect patience as an example to those who were to believe in him for eternal life. (1 Tim. 1:13, 15–16)

Paul believed that God saved him the *way* he did and *when* he did so that people who despaired that they were too sinful to be saved might have hope. God showed mercy to "the foremost" sinner—"a blasphemer, persecutor, and insolent opponent." And Paul makes explicit why God saved him when he was so far gone: to "display his perfect patience as an example to those who were to believe." He saved Paul this way for you. And for me. If God is not patient with us, we are hopeless. But Paul's vulnerability here is for our hope, as we imperfectly pursue holiness.

That a man with Paul's authority and with his exalted role in the church—commissioned by the risen Christ himself—should be this vulnerable with his own imperfections is utterly astonishing. And not only is he open about his imperfections, but he actually turns them for the comfort and encouragement of others. This is not the way of a deluded or a deceptive man. It has the mark of deep, humble inner security and mental health. It is the kind of character I love—and trust.

28

Unrivaled Success as a Missionary, with No Conceit

Paul was one of the most fruitful missionaries in the history of the Christian church. The scope, the sacrifice, and the results have scarcely been paralleled since his day. And yet his boast was relentlessly in Christ and not himself.

Paul was converted to Christ while he was in the process of persecuting Christ. His future partner, the physician Luke, who wrote the narrative of so much of Paul's life, recorded Paul's conversion like this:

> Saul [Paul's Jewish name], still breathing threats and murder against the disciples of the Lord, . . . approached Damascus, and suddenly a light from heaven shone around him. And falling to the ground, he heard a voice saying to him, "Saul, Saul, why are you persecuting me? . . . I am Jesus, whom you are persecuting. But rise and enter the city, and you will be told what you are to do." (Acts 9:1, 3–6)

When he stood up, he was blind. Jesus sent a man named Ananias to open his eyes and explain what was happening. Ananias received these instructions from Jesus:

> Go, for he is a chosen instrument of mine to carry my name before the Gentiles and kings and the children of Israel. For I will show him how much he must suffer for the sake of my name. (Acts 9:15–16)

Later, when Paul reported what happened, he reported more fully the mission he had received from Jesus. Jesus had said to him,

> Rise and stand upon your feet, for I have appeared to you for this purpose, to appoint you as a servant and witness to the things in which you have seen me and to those in which I will appear to you, delivering you from your people and from the Gentiles—to whom I am sending you to open their eyes, so that they may turn from darkness to light and from the power of Satan to God, that they may receive forgiveness of sins and a place among those who are sanctified by faith in me. (Acts 26:16–18)

Launching the Greatest Missionary Life

Thus was launched one of the most courageous, sacrificial, effective missionary careers in the history of the Christian church. Paul discerned in this calling that he was not to be a pastor who lingers long with the churches he starts, but that he was always to be pushing toward the frontiers where there were no Christians. "I make it my ambition to preach the gospel, not where Christ has already been named" (Rom. 15:20).

This ambition to push ever farther into unreached regions explains how Paul could say in his letter to the Roman church:

From Jerusalem and all the way around to Illyricum [to-day's Balkans] I have fulfilled the ministry of the gospel of Christ. . . . Since I no longer have any room for work in these regions, and since I have longed for many years to come to you, I hope to see you in passing as I go to Spain. (Rom. 15:19, 23–24)

Not an Evangelist, Not a Pastor, but a Frontier Missionary

We know for a fact that in those regions of which he says, "I no longer have any room for work," many unbelieving people still need to be evangelized. We know this because Paul left Timothy behind as a pastor in those regions and told him, "Do the work of an evangelist" (2 Tim. 4:5). But Paul did not see himself as an evangelist. An evangelist works where the church has been established, and from the church base tries to win converts among people nearby.

But Paul's calling and ambition was to take the gospel where there were no established churches. This is why I call him a missionary rather than a pastor or an evangelist, even though the term *missionary* is not in the Bible.

In this calling—planting churches in regions where there were none—Paul paid an enormous price of suffering, and he was historically successful. I say *historically* because, by the time his life was over, there were churches from Jerusalem to northern Italy that would endure for centuries of empire-wide significance.

But it's not as though Paul would make converts, start a church, and forget about them as he moved on. Thirteen of the books of the New Testament are witness to Paul's care for those churches. He prayed for them constantly, and he wrote to them. These letters are another tribute to Paul's greatness as a missionary.

All His Fruitfulness a Gift

Nevertheless, in spite of all this success, Paul did not boast in himself. He boasted in Christ. He did not minimize the significance of his work. He did not say, "Oh, it's nothing." It was not nothing! It was glorious. And yet Paul's experience of the power of Christ in his life caused him to realize that all the fruit in his hands was a gift of God:

> In Christ Jesus, then, I have reason to be proud of my work for God. For I will not venture to speak of anything except what Christ has accomplished through me to bring the Gentiles to obedience—by word and deed. (Rom. 15:17–18)

In other words, wonderful things happened through Paul's ministry—things that are worthy of a boast. But the question was, In whom shall Paul boast? His answer was, "Let the one who boasts, boast in the Lord" (1 Cor. 1:31). "Far be it from me to boast except in the cross of our Lord Jesus Christ" (Gal. 6:14). "We . . . glory [that is, boast] in Christ Jesus and put no confidence in the flesh" (Phil. 3:3).

God Gives the Growth

Whether he thought of the planter or the one who waters the seed, Paul made clear why his boast was in the Lord and not in himself or in others:

> What then is Apollos? What is Paul? Servants through whom you believed, as the Lord assigned to each. I planted, Apollos watered, but God gave the growth. So neither he who plants nor he who waters is anything, but only God who gives the growth. (1 Cor. 3:5–7)

Paul knew he had worked hard. He knew he had suffered much. He knew he had been faithful to his Lord. He expressed no artificial humility that denied any of his love and labor. Rather, he held the deep conviction that as he toiled, Christ was working in him and through him with decisive power.

> [Christ] we proclaim, warning everyone and teaching everyone with all wisdom, that we may present everyone mature in Christ. *For this I toil, struggling with all his energy that he powerfully works within me.* (Col. 1:28–29)

Christ Was the Greater Worker in Paul's Work

This was the paradox, the secret, of the Christian life—especially the life of a fruitful missionary. Namely, we toil with all our might, but the toil is most deeply a decisive work of Christ in us. So Paul describes his life: "It is no longer I who live, but Christ who lives in me. And the life I now live in the flesh I live by faith in the Son of God, who loved me and gave himself for me" (Gal. 2:20).

Paul lived by faith day by day, hour by hour, in the help that the living Christ supplies. But faith, by its very nature, is not something we boast in. Faith is the one thing in our heart that directs its dependence outward onto another, not the self. Therefore, a life of dependence on the power of Christ was the key to Paul's beautiful combination of stunning missionary successes along with no boasting in himself.

A Great Life

This is the kind of life I love to watch. If there were no amazing successes, we would be less amazed, less admiring. And the humility would not be so surprising. But when the successes are many, and the cost is high, and the accolades are humbly and happily deflected to Christ, and there is no pretense or sham, then say, "This is a great life! I want to know this man. I want, in some small way, to be like him."

29

The Pursuit of Pure Doctrine and Passion for the Poor

In all his passion for truth and doctrinal maturity, Paul relentlessly carried a practical burden for the poor and sought, throughout his ministry, to include his churches in caring for the poor the way he did.

Paul did not have a romanticized view of the poor. He did not assume poverty makes everyone humble and dependent on God. He had read his Bible—the Old Testament Scriptures: "A poor man who oppresses the poor is a beating rain that leaves no food" (Prov. 28:3). And he probably knew the parable of Jesus that describes a poor slave, who had just been forgiven all his debts, wringing the neck of another poor man (Matt. 18:23–35). So he knew, as the law said, "[You shall not] be partial to a poor man in his lawsuit" (Ex. 23:3).

Paul Knew God Hates Oppression

Paul also knew that the poor are unusually vulnerable to unjust treatment from those who have power and money.

And he knew that God hates that kind of oppression of the weak by the powerful. He knew it from the Old Testament prophets:

> Hear this word, you cows of Bashan . . .
> who oppress the poor, who crush the needy. . . .
> The Lord God has sworn by his holiness
>   that, behold, the days are coming upon you,
> when they shall take you away with hooks.
>   (Amos 4:1–2)

And he knew it from Jesus and the gospel, the same way James did:

> Behold, the wages of the laborers who mowed your fields, which you kept back by fraud, are crying out against you, and the cries of the harvesters have reached the ears of the Lord of hosts. You have lived on the earth in luxury and in self-indulgence. You have fattened your hearts in a day of slaughter. You have condemned and murdered the righteous person. He does not resist you. (James 5:4–6)

Therefore, God had made laws to protect the poor, and his wise men warned against exploitation:

> You shall not oppress a hired worker who is poor and needy, whether he is one of your brothers or one of the sojourners who are in your land within your towns. (Deut. 24:14)

> Whoever oppresses a poor man insults his Maker,
>   but he who is generous to the needy honors him.
>   (Prov. 14:31)

And of course, Jesus treated the poor and the outcast with unprecedented compassion. And he told his followers that they should be constantly openhanded with their fellow Christians who are poor, because what they do to the poor brothers, they do to him:

> The King will say to those on his right, "Come, you who are blessed by my Father, inherit the kingdom prepared for you from the foundation of the world. For I was hungry and you gave me food, I was thirsty and you gave me drink, I was a stranger and you welcomed me, I was naked and you clothed me, I was sick and you visited me, I was in prison and you came to me. . . . Truly, I say to you, as you did it to one of the least of these my brothers, you did it to me." (Matt. 25:34–36, 40)

Apostolic Passion for the Poor

I mention all of this background to show why Paul and the other apostles made caring for the poor a significant priority. When Paul met Peter, James, and John, the big issue was, Will they affirm each other's apostleship? They did. But that was not the only issue. Paul reported that these "pillars" of the early church "asked us to remember the poor." Paul described that task as "the very thing I was eager to do" (Gal. 2:9–10). Eager. Passionate.

So we see scattered through Paul's letters, and through the narrative of his life in the book of Acts, references to his collection for the poor, especially in Jerusalem. All of 2 Corinthians 8–9 is an extended argument that the Corinthian Christians should be as generous in this collection as the churches of Macedonia.

Then in Romans, Paul refers to both of these centers of generosity, saying, "Macedonia and Achaia have been pleased to make some contribution for the poor among the saints at Jerusalem" (Rom. 15:26). And, finally, Luke reports the actual delivery of the funds Paul had been collecting: "Now after several years I came to bring alms to my nation and to present offerings" (Acts 24:17).

Doctrinal Purity and Duty to the Poor

Now, that is beautiful—a man who never loses sight of the needs of the poor. But what makes this unusually attractive to me is that in our own day, there is sometimes, and sadly, a stereotypical distinction between Christian leaders who emphasize caring for the poor and leaders who emphasize doctrinal faithfulness. The lovers of truth and doctrine may suspect that emphasizing care for the poor implies going soft on biblical doctrine. And the lovers of the poor may suspect that emphasizing doctrine makes one indifferent to the needs of the poor. Both of those suspicions have been justified in certain times and places.

So I'm impressed that Paul cannot be squeezed into either of those stereotypes. Paul cared for the souls of his churches with doctrinal help, and he cared for the poor of his churches with material help. Both were prominent. He wrote his doctrinally rich letters to help the churches

> equip the saints for the work of ministry, for building up the body of Christ, until we all attain to the unity of the faith and of the knowledge of the Son of God, to mature manhood, to the measure of the stature of the fullness of Christ, so that we may no longer be children, tossed to and fro by the waves and carried about by every wind of doctrine, by human cunning, by craftiness in deceitful schemes. (Eph. 4:12–14)

He knew that people die a worse death from winds of false doctrine than from the pain of poverty. Physical starvation never damned anybody. But spiritual starvation has brought millions to the grave without hope. Paul would say as strongly as anyone that Christians seek to rescue people from *all* suffering, especially eternal suffering (Eph. 4:28; 2 Thess. 1:9).

The Embodiment of Salvation

So he gave himself to the great doctrinal work of telling the whole truth, and to the great work of compassion in providing for the poor. He brought salvation to the soul and relief to the body. Or better: he brought salvation, and this salvation includes new convictions about reality and new compassion for the hurting. It changes a person forever from selfish to loving—from exploiting to standing up for the exploited.

Paul embodied this salvation. He cannot be easily stereotyped. When I watch him handle the truth for the sake of eternity and handle money for the sake of the hungry, I see something deeply admirable. This is a beautiful combination of conviction and compassion that fills me with admiration for this man.

PART 7

THE BEST GIFT
PAUL COULD GIVE

30

The Greatest Chapter in the Bible and the Most Important Promise in My Life

In "The Great 8"—the eighth chapter of Paul's letter to the Romans—Paul showed the connection between the death of Jesus and the certainty of receiving "all things." In doing so, he gave me my favorite, most sweeping, most hope-supplying verse in the Bible, Romans 8:32.

You come to love a person when what he says penetrates so deeply into your soul that it changes the way you think about everything—and the change is full of hope. That is what I would say Paul did for me when I was awakened to the all-encompassing logic of heaven in Romans 8:32. I was twenty-three years old.

When I saw this verse as I had never seen it before, God implanted it so firmly in my soul that it became a lifelong, living agent of practical, hope-giving, life-altering power. I can't separate that experience from the man who spoke these words.

Of all the places in the Bible that provide a solid place to stand when all around you is shaking, this has been my foundation stone more than any other:

> *He who did not spare his own Son but gave him up for us all, how will he not also with him graciously give us all things?* (Rom. 8:32)

Even Children Understand *a Fortiori* Arguments

Romans 8:32 is a quintessential summary of the argument (and *argument* is the right word!) of the first eight chapters of Paul's letter to the Romans. There is a logic to this greatest of all letters. I call it the logic of heaven.

This kind of logic has a technical name. You may or may not know the name of the logic, but you definitely know how to use it. You can call it an argument, or a logic, from the greater to the lesser. The technical name is *a fortiori*, which is Latin for "from the stronger." The idea is this: if you have exerted your strength to accomplish something *hard*, then surely you can exert your strength to accomplish something *easier*. That's an *a fortiori* argument.

So, suppose you say to your child, "Please run next door and ask Mr. Smith if we can borrow his pliers." But your child says, "But what if Mr. Smith doesn't want us to borrow his pliers?" How can you persuade your child that Mr. Smith will surely loan you his pliers? By using an *a fortiori* argument!

It goes like this. You say to your child, "Yesterday Mr. Smith was happy to let us borrow his car for the day. If he was happy for me to borrow his car, he'll be very willing for us to borrow his pliers." Even children grasp *a fortiori* arguments.

Loaning his car was a greater sacrifice than loaning his pliers. Therefore, it was harder to loan his car than it will be to loan his pliers. If he was inclined to do the harder thing, then he will be willing to do the easier thing. That's the way we use *a fortiori* arguments.

Paul's Fabulous *a Fortiori*

Now watch Paul use this kind of argument for the greatest event in the history of the world. He says, *God did not spare his own Son but gave him up for us all.* That's the harder thing. *Therefore, he will most certainly give us all things with him.* That's the easier thing. When this argument penetrates through the callouses of familiarity, it becomes gloriously hope-filled and all-encompassing.

I had read that verse all my life. But here I was at twenty-three, and for the first time, this logic—this God-inspired logic, this holy, heavenly, glorious, inexhaustible logic—penetrated into my soul and implanted itself so that it became an unshakable foundation and living root of hope and power, a lifelong, living agent of practical, hope-giving, life-altering power. I'll explain why in a moment. But first focus with me for a moment on the content of the two halves of this verse.

The Greatest Obstacle to Our Everlasting Happiness

First, think with me about the first half of Romans 8:32: "*He who did not spare his own Son but gave him up for us all . . .*"

What are the great obstacles between us and everlasting happiness? One obstacle is our sin. We are all sinners (Rom. 3:23), and the wages of that sin is eternal death (Rom. 6:23). Another obstacle is the wrath of God. If God is justly wrathful toward us in our sinful guilt, then we have no hope of everlasting happiness. And Paul leaves no doubt that we are under

God's wrath. We are in fact "children of wrath, like the rest of mankind" (Eph. 2:3).

Those seem to be the biggest obstacles between us and everlasting happiness. But are they? I think there is a bigger obstacle, one that will be much harder to overcome—the one Paul points to in this first half of Romans 8:32. This obstacle is God's infinite love and joy toward the beauty and honor of his own Son.

See if you don't hear this obstacle in the first half of Romans 8:32: "He who *did not spare his own Son* but gave him up for us all . . ." Paul expects us to feel the massive tension between the phrase *his own Son* and the phrase *did not spare*. This is supposed to sound like the hardest thing that was ever done—God's sacrifice of the Son of God. "His *own* Son."

Could God Possibly Hand Over His Only Son?

When Paul calls Jesus God's *own Son*, the point is that there are no others like him, and he is infinitely precious to the Father. Twice while Jesus was on earth God said, "This is my *loved* Son" (Matt. 3:17; 17:5, my translation). In Colossians 1:13, Paul calls him "the Son of his *love*" (my translation).

Jesus himself told the parable of the tenants, in which a master's servants were beaten and killed by the wicked tenants when the servants came to collect the harvest that belonged to the master. The master, amazingly, decides to send his own son to try one more time to collect what was rightly his. Jesus describes this picture of God with these words: "He had still one other, a *loved* son" (Mark 12:6, my translation). One son is all God the Father had. And he loved him infinitely.

The point of Romans 8:32 is that this love of God for his one and only Son was like a massive, Mount Everest obstacle standing between God and our salvation. Here was an obstacle almost insurmountable. Could God—would God—overcome his

cherishing, admiring, treasuring, white-hot, infinite, affection-
ate bond with his Son and hand him over to be lied about and
betrayed and denied and abandoned and mocked and flogged
and beaten and spit on and nailed to a cross and pierced with a
sword, like an animal being butchered and hung up on a rack?

God Did Not Spare Him but Sent Him

Would he really do that? If he would, then we could know with
full certainty that whatever goal he was pursuing on the other
side of that obstacle *could never fail*. There could be no greater
obstacle. So whatever he was pursuing is as good as done.

The unthinkable reality that Romans 8:32 affirms is that
God did it. He did hand him over. God *did not* spare him. You
might say, Didn't Judas hand him over (Mark 3:19)? Didn't Pilate hand him over (Mark 15:15)? Didn't Herod and the mobs
of people hand him over (Acts 4:27–28)? Worst of all, didn't *we*
hand him over (1 Cor. 15:3; Gal. 1:4; 1 Pet. 2:24)? And perhaps
most surprisingly, didn't Jesus hand himself over (John 10:17;
19:30)? The answer to all those questions is yes.

But in Romans 8:32 Paul is penetrating through all these
agents, all these instruments, of death. He is saying the most
unthinkable thing: in and behind and beneath and through all
these human agents, God was handing over his Son to death.
"This Jesus [was] delivered up according to the definite plan
and foreknowledge of God" (Acts 2:23). In Judas and Pilate and
Herod and the crowds and the Gentile soldiers and our sin and
Jesus's lamb-like submission, God himself handed over his Son.
Nothing greater or harder has ever happened. Or ever will.

The Easy Half of the Argument

Therefore, in Paul's *a fortiori* argument, God has done the
hardest thing to give us everlasting happiness. He did not spare

his own Son but gave him up for us all. What does this guarantee? Paul puts it in the form of a rhetorical question (that means a question he expects us to immediately answer correctly): "*how will he not also with him graciously give us all things?*"

Paul expects us to turn this into a strong, certain statement. Namely: "He most certainly will also with him graciously give us all things."

Since God did not spare his own Son but gave him up for us all, therefore he will most certainly give us all things with him.

All things! This is not a promise of a trouble-free life. Four verses later Paul says, "For your sake we are being killed all the day long; we are regarded as sheep to be slaughtered" (Rom. 8:36).

"He will give us *all things*" means *all things* we need to do his will. *All things* we need to glorify him. *All things* we need to move from predestined to called to justified to glorified—that is, to everlasting happiness (Rom. 8:30).

Since God did not spare his own Son, but gave him up for us all, therefore

- all things will work together for our good (v. 28).
- we will be conformed to the image of his Son (v. 29).
- we will be glorified (v. 30).
- no one can successfully be against us (v. 31).
- no charge shall stick against us (v. 33).
- nothing can separate us from the love of Christ (v. 35).
- in tribulation and distress and persecution and famine and nakedness and danger and sword, we are more than conquerors (vv. 35–37).
- neither death nor life, nor angels nor rulers, nor things present nor things to come, nor powers, nor height nor depth, nor anything else in all creation, will be able to

separate us from the love of God in Christ Jesus our Lord (vv. 38–39).

All My Hope Hangs on the Logic of Romans 8:32

Now we circle back to the beginning. I said that when I was twenty-three, this logic of heaven penetrated so deeply into my soul that it changed the way I think about everything—and that the change was full of hope. What I meant was this. This logic of heaven teaches that the Father's not sparing the Son secures every promise I have ever trusted in, or ever will.

I live my life every day by the promises of God. I owe every one of them to the logic of Romans 8:32. Do you see how sweeping and all-encompassing this is for me? All my hope hangs on God's promises. And all the promises (all things) are guaranteed by the logic of Romans 8:32.

Paul said, "All the promises of God find their Yes in [Jesus]" (2 Cor. 1:20). That is because the Father did not spare his Son. He did it so that *all things*—all these promises—would be absolutely certain for those who trust him. I have fought all the battles of my life with the promises of God—battles against fear and lust and greed and pride and anger. Battles for courage and purity and contentment and humility and peace and love. All of them by the word of God—the promises of God.

Behind every one of those battles is the logic of heaven: "I did not spare my own Son; therefore, my promise to you cannot fail. I will help you. Go. Do what I have called you to do." The logic of heaven is all encompassing, all pervading, all precious. And what shall I feel for the man who showed me these things? Shall I not love him? God knows I love him.

A Final Commendation

Paul's Christ-Embodying Love for Me

My aim has been to help you along the way in getting to know the apostle Paul and what he taught and how he lived. Behind this aim is the hope and prayer that this man's God-entranced soul and his unparalleled vision of Jesus Christ and the authenticity of his life would move you to admire him and believe his message and embrace his Lord.

Paul has won my trust. I cannot see him as a deceiver or as one who is deceived. In the man and his teaching I am confronted with a crisis—a huge crisis that determines the meaning of my life and the destiny of my soul. Paul said that a day of judgment is coming for all the world. And on that day, he said, "according to my gospel, God judges the secrets of men by Christ Jesus" (Rom. 2:16).

When I consider my life and the secret sins of my heart—the defective motives of selfishness that have polluted every deed I have ever done—I feel dread and hopelessness at the prospect of judgment before an infinitely holy God, who said that the wages of sin is death (Rom. 6:23). Paul has shown me that this fear is wise and well-founded. "Do not become proud, but fear" (Rom. 11:20). So my crisis is real. Paul knew it. And he approved it. He is a good doctor and does not make light of terminal illness.

He is honest. And like his Master, he loves me. Though he has never seen me, he has diagnosed my hopeless, sinful condition before God. He has looked me in the eye and told me the truth. There is no hope in myself. And then, through a life of almost unremitting suffering, he has labored to show me and teach me where there is relief and life and hope. He put it in the form of a personal testimony to help me feel its preciousness:

> For [Christ's] sake I have suffered the loss of all things and count them as rubbish, in order that I may gain Christ and be found in him, not having a righteousness of my own that comes from the law, but that which comes through faith in Christ, the righteousness from God that depends on faith. (Phil. 3:8–9)

Here is the dawning of the light of hope for the darkness of my dread, a righteousness that is not my own! A righteousness that is from God, not myself. Yet a righteousness that would count as mine, if I could be found *in Christ.* And how might I be found *in Christ?* Not by law-keeping, but by faith. It is a righteousness "which comes through *faith* in Christ, the righteousness from God that depends on *faith.*" Which means that at the last judgment, Christ would be my advocate, not my adversary.

Martin Luther said that if this news were true, he would stand on his head for joy. I suspect he kept his word, and all of Wittenberg leaped with gladness as Paul's gospel turned the world upside down.

Three times Paul said, "I am not lying":

I am speaking the truth in Christ—*I am not lying*; my conscience bears me witness in the Holy Spirit. (Rom. 9:1)

The God and Father of the Lord Jesus, he who is blessed forever, knows that *I am not lying.* (2 Cor. 11:31)

For this I was appointed a preacher and an apostle (I am telling the truth, *I am not lying*), a teacher of the Gentiles in faith and truth. (1 Tim. 2:7)

He said this with such earnestness because he knew that if we rejected him as a true spokesman of the risen Christ, we would be rejecting all hope at the last day. Paul felt the weight of this. He knew the connection between his own truthfulness and what it would mean for his readers to reject him as a liar or deceiver.

I can see him looking at me with tears in his eyes (Rom. 9:2; 10:1; Phil. 3:18). And I hear him say to me very personally, "I did not burden anyone. . . . And why? Because I do not love you? God knows I do!" (see 2 Cor. 11:9, 11).

Yes. He does. In this love he is the embodiment of the love of Christ—for me. So to use the words of another apostle, John: The essential thing is not that I love Paul, but that Paul loved me, and showed me the love of Christ who loved us both and gave himself for us (see 1 John 4:10). That has made all the difference.

General Index

Scripture Index

❊ desiringGod

Everyone wants to be happy. Our website was born and built for happiness. We want people everywhere to understand and embrace the truth that God is *most glorified in us when we are most satisfied in him*. We've collected more than thirty years of John Piper's speaking and writing, including translations into more than forty languages. We also provide a daily stream of new written, audio, and video resources to help you find truth, purpose, and satisfaction that never end. And it's all available free of charge, thanks to the generosity of people who've been blessed by the ministry.

If you want more resources for true happiness, or if you want to learn more about our work at Desiring God, we invite you to visit us at desiringGod.org.

desiringGod.org

Also Available from John Piper

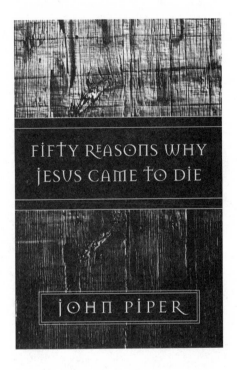

John Piper gathered fifty reasons from the New Testament to answer the most important question that each of us must face: What did Jesus accomplish through the cross for sinners?

For more information, visit **crossway.org**.